ESCAPE
ADULTHOOD

ESCAPE ADULTHOOD

8 Secrets from Childhood for the Stressed-Out Grown-Up

Jason W. Kotecki

JBiRD iNK, Limited
Madison, Wisconsin

This book may be purchased for educational, business, or sales promotional use. Quantity discounts available.

Printed in the United States of America.

First Paperback Edition

Library of Congress Control Number: 2005903443

Publisher's Cataloging-In-Publication Data
(Prepared by The Donohue Group, Inc.)

Kotecki, Jason W.
  Escape adulthood : 8 secrets from childhood for the stressed-out grown-up / Jason W. Kotecki. -- 1st paperback ed.

  p. : ill. ; cm.
  Includes bibliographical references.
  ISBN-13: 978-0-9715253-3-7
  ISBN-10: 0-9715253-3-1

1. Stress management. 2. Life skills. 3. Adjustment (Psychology) 4. Adjustment (Psychology) in children. 5. Motivation (Psychology) I. Title.

RA785 .K68 2005
155/.904/2   2005903443

*This book is dedicated to my wife Kim,
who has the amazing ability to look like a million bucks
and live like a six-year-old.*

Delight in the Little Things
Dream Big
Get Curious
Live Passionately
Play
Be Honest
Have Faith
Maintain Perspective

Table of Contents

Preface   ix
Acknowledgements   xiii
Introduction   15
Delight in the Little Things   25
Dream Big   45
Get Curious   65
Live Passionately   83
Play   101
Be Honest   117
Have Faith   137
Maintain Perspective   157
Conclusion   175
Endnotes   177
About the Author   187

Preface

Perhaps you've read the following resignation from adult-hood. It has been around the world countless times via e-mail forward, and the author is anonymous:

To Whom It May Concern:

I am hereby officially tendering my resignation as an adult. I have decided I would like to accept the responsi-bilities of a 6-year-old again. I want to go to McDonald's and think that it's a four-star restaurant. I want to sail sticks across a fresh mud puddle and make a sidewalk with rocks. I want to think M&Ms are better than money because you can eat them. I want to play kickball during recess and paint with watercolors in art. I want to lie under a big oak tree and run a lemonade stand with my friends on a hot summer's day.

I want to return to a time when life was simple, when all you knew were colors, multiplication tables, and nursery rhymes; but that didn't bother you, because you didn't know what you didn't know and you didn't care. All you knew was to be happy because you were blissfully unaware of all the things that should make you worried or upset. I want to think the world is fair. That everyone is honest and good. I want to believe that anything is possible. I want to be oblivious to the complexities of life and be overly excited by the little things again. I want to live simply again. I don't want my day to consist of computer crashes, mountains of paperwork, depressing news, how to survive more days in the month than there is money in the bank, doctor bills, gossip, illness, and loss of loved ones. I want to believe in the power of smiles, hugs, a kind word, truth, justice, peace, dreams, the imagination, mankind, and making angels in the snow. So...here are my checkbook and my car keys, my credit card bills and my 401K statements. I am officially resigning from adulthood. And if you want to discuss this further, you'll have to catch me first, 'cause...

...Tag! You're it.

I wrote this book because I can certainly relate to this particular proclamation. And judging by how many times it's been in and out of people's e-mail boxes, I think I can assume it strikes a chord with a good many people. Who wouldn't want to recapture those innocent times we took for granted, to be free from the responsibilities that burden us as adults? I wrote this book because the whole idea seemed like a good one.

But I also wrote this book to address the reality of our situation. Let's face it: No matter how hard we try, we're never going to be six again. Ever. And we can all agree that it wouldn't be very wise to discard all responsibilities and stop paying our bills. Furthermore, we would be doing a great disservice to others if we acted blissfully unaware of the world around us, because, believe it or not, there is a great benefit in growing up and becoming an adult. That's right! We finally have the power to do something about the problems we have come to see around us. It doesn't do anyone any good to dwell aimlessly on an idealized return to childhood, but I think it is very worthwhile to spend some time thinking of how we can bring some of those long-lost childhood ideals back into our lives. We just need to escape the adulthood we've created for ourselves.

Frankly, many of the ills and worries we wish to be disconnected from are actually in our lives of our own choosing. As adults, we have the power within us to make a difference in our own lives and the lives of others, to change the things that dissatisfy us so much about adulthood.

The truth is that we can still get Happy Meals at McDonalds, play kickball, paint with watercolors, and lie under a big oak tree. We can still be overly excited by the little things. We can still believe that anything is possible. We can live simply again. We can still believe in the power of smiles, hugs, a kind word, truth, justice, peace, dreams, imagination, mankind, and making angels in the snow.

I wrote this book because, somewhere along the line, we just forgot how.

Acknowledgements

I would like to thank the Academy...and since I have a few moments before the curtain comes down and we head to commercial break, I'd also like to thank:

Everyone who has inspired and encouraged me to chase my dreams, including Dan & Connie Kotecki, Doug & Katie Kotecki, Virginia Kotecki, Ruth Pittman, Aunt Sarah, Aunt Julie, Uncle Doc, Kristy Halm, Gene & Karen Lamis, Kathi & Troy Hurt, Gene & Dorothy Koneiczka, Mrs. Smith, Kathy Yerly, Pat Tutaj, Diana Garrett, Joelyn Bednarik, Megan Moritz, Teresa Bloomquist, my Peterstown TEC family, Ken & Jyll Pozzi, Dan & Katie Wujek, Ryan Hall, John Wentz, Jennifer D'Souza, Fr. Steve, Joanne Mangun, Mike & Michelle Clark, Matt Tipperreiter, Mary Sue Seibert-Frett, Carlo & Darlene Colosimo, Matt & Gina Goodbred, Tim & Renée Tiemann, Betty Repsel, Vicki Tomaszewski, Rick Crespo, Jacqui Sakowski, Bob Pelletier, Pete Cymbalak, Marilyn Schoberg, Allan Dash, Chris Hollenback, Michelle Alswager, and anyone else my stupid little brain has left out. I will try to repay you by sharing your kind light of encouragement with as many people as I can.

Thanks, Pat. Your red pen simultaneously transported me back to high school English and made this book better.

Thanks, Kira. Your professional eye was priceless.

Thanks, Jenna. Your dedication to this cause humbles me.

Thanks, Sue. That little retreat we led long ago was just the beginning. Thanks for walking this road with me.

Thanks, Jaimie. Without your nudge, this book might still only exist in my head.

Thanks, Gary and Joyce. Your example has been invaluable and your prayers have been priceless.

Thanks, Mom. You taught me that it takes more than just a head in the clouds to make dreams come true.

Thanks, Dad. You taught me the power of persistence.

Thanks, Kim. You're the bestest friend ever.

Thanks, Jesus. You never cease to amaze me.

Introduction

"Grown-ups never understand anything for themselves, and it is tiresome for children to be always and forever explaining things to them."

Antoine de Saint-Exupery

Remember childhood? Remember when meetings were held under a tent made of couch cushions and blankets, and candy was worth more than any mutual fund? If you think really hard, I bet you can. When we were kids, we had an innate ability to tackle life head on. Everything seemed so simple and uncomplicated. Although *we* were messy, life didn't seem to be. As children, we each held the secret answers to a happy, fulfilled life. The bad news is that when we grew up, most of us completely forgot those answers.

What the heck happened? If things were so great and we had such a wonderful way of handling life, why did we ever abandon these little nuggets of wisdom?

Here's what I think we should blame it on: puberty. Adolescence and puberty were stages that shockingly and uncomfortably tore us from the simplicity of childhood into the complexity of adulthood, and I don't think any of us wants to relive that portion of our lives. (High school gym class, anyone?) Perhaps in our rush to actually get beyond the uncertainty and uncomfortable horror of that phase, we quickly embraced all that adulthood had to offer. When we were kids, being grown-up seemed so fun and exciting and mysterious. "Adulthood" was like a secret land filled with boundless opportunities, every one of them off-limits to kids. As children, we spent a lot of time playing dress-up, imagining what we would be. We couldn't wait to shave, drive, date, and drink beer. Then, eager to get past the pimples and awkward points of puberty, we cast aside everything that was childish in order to be accepted as grown-up. And in this process, we begin to lose sight of the secrets that we once knew by heart. The reality and responsibilities of life begin to weigh on us, and the burdens of work, bills, and family life cover over these childlike traits. We become jaded, dull, disillusioned, and depressed, with super-high stress levels. We suddenly have too much to do, but never enough energy to get it all done. This condition is called "Adultitis."

ADULTITIS

A common condition occurring in people between the ages of 21–121, marked by chronic dullness, mild depression, moderate to extremely high stress levels, a general fear of change, and, in some extreme case, the inability to smile. Patients can appear aimless, discontent, and anxious about many things. Onset can be accelerated by an excess burden of bills, overwhelming responsibilities, or a boring work life. Generally, individuals in this condition are not fun to be around.

It doesn't take long before we all come to a realization: adulthood sure isn't what it was cracked up to be. It's way more complicated than advertised. Technology was supposed to make our lives easier. Perhaps it has, to some degree, but can I get a show of hands from anyone whose life is simpler? Or who has more time on their hands thanks to this blazing technology? Anybody?

Things like e-mail and junk mail, deadlines and divorce, mortgage payments and car payments, taxes and heart attacks, have dampened all of the unbridled fun we were supposed to have when we grew up. The whole "living on your own" and "living by your *own* rules" dream hardly materialized the way that we imagined it would.

But where is it written that we need to succumb to all of these external pressures and be so serious all the time? Most of us will agree that life *can* be just a tad overwhelming at times. I mean, wouldn't it be nice to go back to the days of afternoon naps with a warm homemade cookie waiting for you when you woke up? Those days are long gone. Or are they? Is there a way to actually escape this thing called "adulthood" and return to childhood?

That's where the good news comes in. I think there are eight ways to escape "adulthood." You see, these traits from childhood are not the exclusive property of children. They are inherent in all of us, placed there by our loving Creator. It's kind of like how birds have natural instincts built in that remind them to fly south for the winter, and where to look for worms. Birds depend on these instincts to live. We, too, have certain natural instincts that help us to live our lives to the fullest. All children have them. We're born with them. They come naturally, and they never really go away, even if they're a bit rusty.

> These childlike instincts come naturally, and they never really go away, even if they're a bit rusty.

For some people, they're *really* rusty.

Throughout this book, I'll be discussing the eight qualities that all children are born with, and you'll see how you can dust them off and start using them again. Once you do this, you'll begin to see some immediate changes in your life.

Besides having a lot more fun, you'll break free from the stress of the high-paced rat race to find *real* happiness. You'll make a profound difference in the lives of people around you. You will accomplish things in your life that you once thought were impossible, while uncovering opportunities to solve unsolvable problems. What's more, you'll melt away built-up stress and fatigue, becoming more energized and productive at home and at work. By resurrecting these childlike traits, you'll be able to gain peace of mind about the things that worry you most, and overcome your greatest fears and challenges. It may be hard to believe, but it's all true. This book is filled with examples of people who've done just that.

I was abundantly blessed with a great childhood experience. I grew up in a middle-class home in a small midwestern town of ten thousand. My dad worked hard as a carpenter and at a lumberyard, and my mom worked hard as a mom at home. I enjoyed lazy summers with my brothers playing baseball in the park and swimming in those little plastic pools. We didn't get everything we wanted, but we had everything we needed. Outside, I went on dangerous missions as Han Solo, explored the ravine behind our house, and created extravagant snow forts in the front yard. It is these experiences that I've been able to draw from to create my comic strip, *Kim & Jason*.

I first drew the characters Kim and Jason when I started dating a girl named, you got it, Kim. She had an amazing childlike spirit that captivated me right from the start. The start happened to be Christmas caroling, and she was wearing red thermal underwear under reindeer boxer shorts with a Santa hat and combat boots—plus, she was cute. So, needless to say, she stood out. Being an artist—the poor, starving kind at the time—I used some old childhood photos and sketched cartoon versions of us. They were a big hit, so I kept it up. Before long, I started getting positive responses from other people, strangers even, and I decided to begin developing a comic strip that celebrated those unique qualities that all children share. Since then, the characters have taken on lives of their own, and the strip has evolved into a microcosm of childhood, offering readers a brief respite from the harried perplexity of adulthood.

The number one question people ask any cartoonist is invariably, "How do you come up with your ideas?" Many people assume that because my wife has been a kindergarten teacher, she provides me with an abundance of ideas for the strip. Perhaps surprisingly, nothing could be further from the truth. Kim often tells me stories about the goings-on with her students; but as far as I can remember, I have never gotten any strip ideas directly from her. Other people assume I must have children from whom I derive inspiration. As of this writing, I do not have any children. I usually crack some joke about the benefits of Mountain Dew or buying ideas on eBay, and sometimes I'll even concede that having a wife as a kindergarten teacher is not a bad thing. Why do I do that? I suppose because there are no easy answers. I wonder if people always ask Michael Jordan how he got to be so good at basketball? Sure, he worked hard to be the best; but a big chunk of his ability was something he was just born with. Above and beyond my fairly idyllic upbringing and creative talents, I believe one of my gifts[1] is the ability to see life from a childlike perspective. I can't explain it, really, but when I put my characters into a situation, I just instinctively know how they would act or what they would be thinking. I guess you could call it a talent; but if I weren't able to utilize it as a cartoonist, I'm not really sure where else it would come in handy. The best way to describe it would be that if my head were a radio, the station would be tuned into childhood and the tuning knob would be missing.

Even my favorite story from the Bible has to do with childhood. It's one of the times Jesus is hanging out with His pals. I don't imagine He was signing autographs (could you imagine what THAT would be worth?), but I'm sure everybody was clamoring to hear and be a part of all of the miraculous and important things that followed this man around like white on rice. Then a little child approached, perhaps pulled like a magnet to this easy-going guy who smiled a lot and seemed to be so much fun. Of course, as grown-ups are prone to do, the disciples admonished the little kid, probably starting off on some lecture about how "the grown-ups are talking, we're busy, now go play." (I've heard that more than a few times in my life.) But then, surprisingly for all who were present, Jesus admonished *them*.

I imagine Him bringing the child close, running His fingers through his hair, and looking deeply into the eyes of the disciples around Him. Then He said, "I tell you the truth, the kingdom of heaven belongs to such as these. Unless you embrace the kingdom of God like a little child, you will never enter it."[2]

Wow... *never?*

That is unquestionably my favorite Bible verse, one that has inspired me for years. On the surface it's quite a challenge and something to think about. What does it mean? Does it mean we're supposed to shirk all responsibility and skip work to go build snow forts? Start paying our bills with Monopoly money? Begin limiting our diets to chicken nuggets and macaroni and cheese?

Just a wild guess, but I'm thinking that *wasn't* His intent. I've spent a long time pondering those words, and I've spent a long time observing kids, trying to figure out exactly what He meant. I've discovered that children have a lot of wonderful things to teach us. Some are obvious, like the idea that it's probably not a very good idea to stick things up our nose or in our ear.[3] But, after much reflection, I've been able to nail down eight really important qualities that kids naturally exhibit. They are the traits that I think Jesus had in mind when He issued the challenge over 2,000 years ago to His friends. The very same challenge He issues to us today.

These are things I've incorporated into *Kim & Jason*, and things I think are important to dwell on. I believe they are hidden keys to live more fruitful, less stressed, more enjoyable lives. Hidden within children are almost magical universal secrets, hinted at by Jesus long ago, and, thankfully, still planted (sometimes deeply) within us.

This book is my humble take on what Jesus was talking about. My hope is that it might shed some light on your life and enable you to get more out of it. In each chapter, I share some anecdotes from my childhood, as well as some observations of children, to bring alive the eight secrets I've uncovered. I know that some of you may be a bit skeptical and perhaps worried that I'll encourage you to quit your job and muck around with

Play-Doh all day long. With that in mind, I've also included many stories of real live grown-ups who have exhibited these time-tested childhood qualities and have enjoyed a measure of success that exceeds anyone's standard.

As you read, these secrets should start to make a lot of sense; because, remember, they're already inside of you. Just like a mother's natural desire to care for her young, these traits were baked in from the very beginning. And even if your childhood was less than stellar, or downright horrible, don't despair. Sadly, due to circumstances beyond our control, not everyone is fortunate enough to fully develop all of these qualities throughout their entire childhood. Abuse, poverty, tragedy, and neglect are just a few of the things that cause children to grow up way too fast, resulting in some of these values to be hidden or neglected. But they are never destroyed. They are always there, waiting to be discovered and utilized. Who says we can't have a second childhood? One that's even better than the first! As I said earlier, these hidden qualities are not exclusive to children. In fact, throughout this book, you'll see examples of people of all ages who have embraced these ideals and become extremely successful, living happy and fulfilled lives. You'll see that Adultitis is completely curable.

Adultitis is completely curable.

Let me take this opportunity to admit that I hate books that provide tons of idealistic theory but no "meat." Ideas are great and all, but they are useless unless acted upon. That's why, besides explaining the eight concepts in depth, my prescription for Adultitis includes 88 real-world, practical, and tangible ways to begin incorporating some of these ideals into your life right away. Today.

I am well aware that no matter how well I've arranged the words on the page, I can't *make* you do anything. The step to a more fun, more fulfilled, less stressed existence is entirely up to you. I pray that this book will be your spark. Above all, I hope you'll find this book to be entertaining, encouraging, and a little inspiring as well.

I am fond of a story about a young girl having lunch with an older friend. They could overhear an argument between two people sitting near them, and the younger girl proclaimed that she could help them get along with each other. Surprised, and keenly interested, the friend asked for some clarification. "You see," said the little girl, "I'm little. The littler you are, the more you know. Little babies know everything, and when you grow up, you get stupider and stupider. It's too bad that they have to fight, but they're old and stupid and can't help it."

Without further ado, let's discover the cure for Adultitis by uncovering the eight secrets from childhood, and end the stupidity.

Note: I have a propensity to make asides when I write. Lots of them. Rather than muddle the main text with mildly interesting thoughts that have very little to do with the actual points I'm trying to make, I've included them in the endnote section at the, um, end.

Delight in the Little Things

"Enjoy the little things, for one day you may look back and realize they were the big things."

Robert Brault

Pizza Hut® is the best restaurant in the history of the world. Or at least it was when I was a kid. I was utterly enchanted by the entire experience that was Pizza Hut. It was a rare occasion when we'd make the trip out to dinner as a family. It usually coincided with the attainment of one of those "Book-It" certificates that schoolchildren earn by reading a certain number of books. One certificate was good for one free personal pan pizza. But my favorite was thin and crispy, so my mom would usually get the individual one for herself.

I was enthralled with the whole experience of the place. Not just the perfect, crispy-crusted pizza, but also how the sausage tasted way better than anything on the frozen pizzas I was accustomed to. I thought it was so awesome: the dark woodwork and dimmed lighting, the red and white checked tablecloth, the red glasses filled with syrupy soft drinks, and the waitresses with those classy visors. Without a doubt, Pizza Hut was a real treat.

I know it sounds cheesy (pun absolutely intended), but I still love going to Pizza Hut. My perspective on the level of ritziness has corrected itself, but I still get a thrill every time I go out to eat. My parents kept a close eye on their money; going out to eat was a treat, not the norm. Even getting a McDonald's Happy Meal was a great event, because it was cheaper for my mom to buy us boys each a cheeseburger and have us share a bag of fries.[1]

I am very grateful for those experiences from my youth, because, intended or not, my parents helped instill in me an appreciation for the little things in life. For many kids, both then and now, eating out at restaurants and indulging in Happy Meals is boring and commonplace. Somehow, over twenty years later, I still get a little rush of excitement every time I sit down at a Pizza Hut. The emotion is only slightly less intensified now that I have a little bit more control over when I get to go.

Our society has become so consumer-driven and materialistic that it doesn't take much for us to get sucked up into wanting to move on to the next big thing, or the rewarding new elaborate experience, hardly taking the time to appreciate the present moment. It's easy to grow discontented with our current situation when there is something newer, bigger, faster out there.

Children aren't so materialistic, however, as illustrated in a story I once heard about a father who became very angry with his young daughter. It was around Christmas time, and he found her wasting a roll of shiny wrapping paper in an attempt to wrap a box. He scolded her terribly, for money was tight, and they could not afford to be wasting things. He became embarrassed the next day when the little girl presented him with the gift—she had wrapped it just for him. But his patience was tested again when he opened the gift only to find an empty box. "Don't you know that when you give someone a present, there's supposed to be something inside?" The daughter looked up at him, tears welling up in her eyes, and said, "But Daddy, there is something inside. Yesterday I blew kisses into the box. They're all for you." Kids seem to more easily grasp the importance of little things, things that aren't really *things*.

Perhaps I've had more time to reflect on this than most of my peers because the road to success for *Kim & Jason* has been long, arduous, and in the early going, penniless. I guess you could say it has been relatively *thingless*. While friends started families, went on tropical vacations, and built nice homes, Kim and I were shopping at discount grocery stores, rotating our meat selection between frozen ground beef and frozen chicken breasts (because the other meats were too expensive), and putting up with our neighbors' loud music and screaming kids in an apartment that was overtaken by greeting card spinners and big boxes of *Kim & Jason* catalogs. (Seriously, given all of the products that populated our living space, I now know what it is like to watch TV and have family dinners in a Hallmark store, as if I ever wanted to.) There were many inconveniences and frustrations, but most of them only surfaced when I got distracted and started comparing my situation with that of others. And that, my friend, is not a vicious cycle you want to venture into. There is *always* somebody better off than you.

It is helpful to gain perspective by considering that there is always someone *worse* off than you, too. In many cases, MUCH worse. The grace of God and my involvement with The Make-A-Wish Foundation®[2] (more on that later) are what have really helped keep me grounded. I've realized that I have a lot to be thankful for, and that fact, combined with the lessons passed down from my parents, has helped me to embrace the importance of appreciating the little things.

Little things are big deals.

One more day is a big deal to parents whose seven-year-old son is dying of cancer. The ability to hear music is a big deal to the conductor who has become deaf. A Happy Meal is a big deal to a child who doesn't know where his next meal will come from. An old apartment overrun by packing boxes and product displays is a big deal to someone who is homeless.

I've found that children have much to teach us in the way of appreciating the little things. Ask any new parent about the joy a baby gets when she first discovers her feet. They may be little feet, but they're a BIG deal. Now it is true that some children seem to be caught in the trap of always wanting something bigger, better, and flashier. I submit that they are that way because of learned behavior from the parents.

My family took a fair number of vacations when I was young. When I say vacations, I'm not talking about European jaunts or Disney World adventures. No, these vacations never extended more than a few hundred miles from home, usually lasted no more than a long weekend, and often involved a discount motel with a loud air conditioner and an overheated pool.

And we loved them! They were a break from the routine, a chance to see something new, and an opportunity to go out to eat in fancy restaurants...like Pizza Hut. I'm not sure how I was able to have so much fun on these budget-friendly road trips, while some kids find themselves bored at Disneyland. Perhaps it is simply because the latter are conditioned to look to the next thing.

Recently, my parents treated my brothers and me to a family vacation in Door County, Wisconsin. Everyone went —my two brothers, our significant others, my brother's two daughters—ten of us in all. It was nice, because we stayed in a big house on Lake Michigan and were free to come and go as we pleased, not restricted to doing everything as a group. There were certainly lots of things to command our attention, but I am certain that the best part for everyone was our nightly bonfires. It was a time when we all came together, recounting the day's adventures, watching the stars come out, and eating novelty jelly beans that tasted like earwax and earthworms.[3] The entire week, including those nightly fireside chats, is a memory we will all carry with us forever. It is a recent reminder in my life of just how important those little things are.

One of my favorite movies is *City of Angels*, starring Meg Ryan and Nicolas Cage. In it, an angel named Seth falls in love with a human and then takes "the fall"—gives up his angelic powers—to become human so he can be with her. The most captivating theme of the movie for me is not the theology within it, but how it portrays this angel experiencing the emotions and sensations of human life for the first time. They are the little things that we have taken for granted because we don't know any different. Seth is taken by all of the sensuality life has to offer—the shower's darting warm water cascading over skin, and the tart, tasty crunchiness of a fresh pear. When contemplating whether or not to take the fall to be with this human being, Seth says, "I'd rather have one breath of her hair, one touch from her hand, one kiss from her warm lips than an eternity without." One breath. One touch. One kiss. Three little things with eternal importance.

I was in college when I first saw the movie. It was a matinee and I remember walking back to the dorm with the day's sun a few hours from fading into the horizon. It was as if my eyes had been opened to things that just a few hours before had been much less than an afterthought. Whether it's the smell of smoky air from the late-summer barbeque, the preciseness of a single blade of grass, or the purity and peace put forth from a baby's smile, the little things are where true joy in life is hidden.

Life is a blessing. To become awakened to and get caught up in the mundane details and hidden surprises that often get lost in the ebb and flow of our days are among the greatest blessings life has to offer. Children see every day as a new adventure, an opportunity for great discoveries, be they large or small. Like Seth the angel, kids are routinely surprised by how cool life is. It is not uncommon for them to be absolutely THRILLED by such things as a lightning bug in captivity, the intricacies of a snowflake, and the giddiness of taking a bubble bath. They're turned on by helium balloons, bedtime stories, and cereal box prizes.

My wife Kim was a kindergarten teacher, so she got to see things through kids' eyes every day. Kindergarten seems to be filled with little things that take on spectacularly gargan-

tuan proportions. Every St. Patrick's Day, some mischievous leprechaun plays havoc in the kindergarten room and leaves mysterious notes all over the place. Green footprints (made of construction paper) are left behind. The kids conspire to build a trap out of blocks and toys. The leprechaun destroys the trap and trashes the room, but not before he leaves some gold behind (Hershey's Kisses wrapped in gold foil). By the time it's over, it escalates into quite a big deal.

In kindergarten, the hundredth day of school is a BIG DEAL. Big enough to warrant a party complete with candy, cookies, and chocolate cake.

Losing your first tooth commonly occurs during kindergarten. THAT is a BIG DEAL. The Tooth Fairy and her satchel of shiny coins make it so.

Planting seeds into a little cup filled with soil is fun, but it's a BIG DEAL when that little seed sprouts and pokes its head up through the dirt.

To a kindergartner, every day brings with it a possibility of something exciting happening. Things that may seem ho-hum and everyday to us are BIG DEALS to them. Is it that they have so many more things to experience, or is it more a matter of perspective?

It is the little things that can impact and enrich a life. I think back to the days when I was five and I'd visit my Grandma K. The things I hold most dear about her and my visits would probably surprise her, as they are not the grandiose gestures of love or the expensive Christmas presents she gave me. In fact, I cannot think of a single Christmas present she ever gave me (and she gave me plenty). Rather, my memories are filled with little things. I remember picking cherries from her tree; she'd use them to make the best pies ever, starting me on a life-long addiction. I remember speeding up and down her backyard sidewalk on a beat-up bike, past the rickety old swing set. I recall sneaking fresh strawberries from her garden, collecting buckeyes from the ground, and pounding out instant classics on her electric organ. When my cousins were over, Grandma would give us full access to her jewelry box so that we could play jewelry store. We spent hours setting up those sparkly riches, then punching our purchases into her antique adding machine, which seemed to weigh more than ten cinder blocks. My grandma always encouraged our imaginations and left us with a treasure chest of wonderful memories. The little things she did stick with me most.

Little things are everywhere, all around us. I love to go to the zoo. Madison, Wisconsin has a really cool free zoo with a good assortment of "big name" animals. By "big name" animals, I'm not talking about two cows, a deer with a broken leg, and some squirrels in a cage. I'm referring to lions, tigers, and bears, with some monkeys, sea lions and giraffes to boot. It is impossible for me to go to the zoo and not come away amazed. I've seen each of these animals what seems like a million times, but I am consistently blown away by the creativity of God in the diversity of the animals He dreamed up. Each one is perfectly designed for whatever it's supposed to do. Why do giraffes have such long necks? To reach the leaves on the tall trees. Why are flamingoes pink? Because of all the shrimp they eat. Why do the lions have such sharp teeth? Mainly because it's awfully hard to gum an antelope to death.

Kim and I routinely go on walks together. She often gives me a hard time because every time we pass a body of water, I'm scanning for fish. I can spot a caterpillar from a block away. And if there is a dead bird or squirrel on the side of the road, I'm certainly going to stop and poke it with a stick. "You're such a little boy," she says.

"Then I must be doing something right," I think, proudly imagining that I'll someday write a book on the topic.

Not that she has much room to talk (although I've never accused her of being a little boy). As I mentioned, one of the first things that attracted me to Kim was her captivating child-like spirit. One of her childlike qualities was her penchant for being easily excited—in a good way. Not only does that take the pressure off a guy (who wants to be with a girl who doesn't bat an eye at a diamond ring because it's not big enough?), but it makes her a very fun person to be around. She has inspired me to let the little boy inside come out and play once in awhile. And, of course, she inspired me to create a certain little comic strip.[4]

I guess it's easier for kids to appreciate the little things, because, in most cases, what other choice do they have? It's not like they have an overly stressful schedule, and they don't have full-time jobs to afford any fancy stuff anyway (unless Mom or Dad over-commit them and sign them up for every extra-curricular activity known to man). But, scheduling issues aside, kids blow us grown-ups away in their ability to notice the little things. Since things are so new to them, children are not hindered by looking at things the way they're "supposed to be." They are not burdened with pre-conceived notions.

One way to take better stock of the little things is to SLOW DOWN. We adults make it hard on ourselves. It's hard to notice the little things when you're running around like a chicken with its head cut off. I really *have* seen chickens run with their heads cut off, and they are, not surprisingly, quite frantic. When you're riding life as if it's a speeding New York subway train, it's gonna be a little hard to notice that every snowflake is different. Many of us arrogantly go around thinking we've seen everything interesting there is to see. With that attitude, it's easy to be closed to the idea that by slowing down, we might notice something we wouldn't see otherwise.

> It's hard to notice the little things when you're running around like a chicken with its head cut off.

Getting out into nature is a great way to reflect on some of the little things in life. There are a few great exercises that will really sharpen your awareness of the little things. First, find a rock or log to sit on. Next, clear your head, close your eyes, and just listen. Before long, even in the most tranquil of settings, you'll hear a chorus of different sounds come forth, sounds that were inaudible just moments ago. Another thing to try is to find a patch of ground and stare at it. Yep, just stare at it—like a staring contest between you and the ground. Pretty soon, you'll see a flurry of activity with small insects scurrying about. In both instances, you've uncovered a hidden world of life that previously didn't seem to exist. All kinds of strange, fascinating, wonderful things are going on right under your nose that were moments ago unnoticeable. That's what happens when you slow down and pay attention to the little things. Did these sounds and creatures just all at once start up when you began paying attention to them? Nope. They've been going on all along, but you were just too distracted to notice.

It may seem overly simple to say that paying more attention to the little things will make such a big impact in your life. Maybe. But living for the next "big thing" and running around like a chicken with your head cut off is not very rewarding either—just ask the chicken. If you're unsatisfied with life, bored, or feel envious of your neighbor, try slowing down and looking around.

When you foster a greater attention to the little things, almost magically, life will become more enjoyable and more exciting. You'll be more appreciative of life, and thankful for what you have. Because of this newfound appreciation, you'll feel less drawn to work like a hamster in a wheel in order to find happiness in a fancier car, or a bigger home, or on a beach somewhere in the Bahamas. Correspondingly, stress levels go down—way down.

> When you foster a greater attention to the little things, almost magically, life will become more enjoyable and more exciting.

A tropical vacation can certainly be fun and rewarding, but real happiness and true rest are found in the beach's breathtaking sunset, rhythmic tides, and the feel of the warm sand. Just think about the wisdom of the little child, who, when asked to recite the Seven Wonders of the World, thoughtfully replied, "To touch, to taste, to see, to hear, to run, to laugh, and to love."

Not long ago, I made myself very proud. Every week, I carve out a few mornings as writing time, when I try to come up with a week's worth of comic gems. I engage in several hours' worth of mental calisthenics as I think, write, edit, think some more, write some more, edit some more...and then edit again and again. I write jokes that will be told to an audience I won't see or hear. I am forced to critically judge my own sense of humor without getting confirmation back on whether or not I have judged wisely. I am grateful that I have Kim to read my finished strip every day, if for no other reason than to validate that what I'm doing is real.

Like any good, self-respecting artist, I typically loathe my past work, especially if it is a year or more old. I am always pushing myself to try to dig even deeper in my writing, exploring more fully each character, and going past my first good idea to the point of trying to make myself laugh out loud. Most of the time, I settle for a chuckle. (As my mom and my wife would testify, I don't get overly excited about things, especially wonderfully thoughtful gifts, but that's another story.)[5]

So I have a good chunk of morning set aside to get the ol' joke factory churning. It can be hard to be creative when you have a deadline that doesn't care whether or not any good strips have emerged. On the morning I'm referring to, I really felt an extra-intense desire to come up with some good stuff. Since it was an absolutely gorgeous day, I grabbed my sketchbooks and iPod and headed off to find inspiration in a park near Lake Monona. Upon settling in at a sturdy wood picnic table with the lapping of waves in front of me, I was happy that I had picked a day when the construction cranes assembling the new shelter weren't echoing behind me. It was peaceful.

Until I looked down at my shirt and noticed a green worm.[6]

Naturally, I was a bit startled (freaked out), and I casually brushed off (frantically swiped away) the harmless (carnivorous) critter. I laughed to myself at how reflexively shook-up I could get over something so small. I went about my writing, but it wasn't long before I noticed that my friend had returned to the table. To my delight, I realized that it was an inchworm (please excuse the lack of scientific terminology). I marveled at how he (or she, if you prefer) made his way along the wooden highway ahead of him. Then, right before my eyes, his color transformed from a bright, light green to a pale brown, blending almost perfectly with that of the table.

Deadlines whispered from the back of my mind, so I got back to work and jotted down some more ideas. But curiosity got the best of me, and I turned my head a little later to see where my new friend was now. I couldn't find him anywhere, speculating that he must have turned on the afterburners. But out of the corner of my eye, I caught a glimpse of the worm, seemingly dangling in mid-air. Upon further inspection, I could see that he was descending from the table via a thin, web-like strand coming from his butt (more confusing bio-speak). It was pretty windy that morning, but that web held strong as he casually descended. I paused in awe to watch this miniscule marvel complete his patient plunge and get on with his day.

Shortly thereafter it was time to pack it up, and as I walked back to the car, I smiled. I was happy and proud that I could still be amazed by the little things, a very childlike quality. My wish is that I will still have that capacity when I'm 90. Interestingly, those five minutes really made my day. And perhaps not ironically, it was a pretty productive one at that.

The next time you're around children, pay close attention to them. Notice how excited they are to find a penny on the ground (even more so when they get to throw it into a fountain). Pay attention to how excited they become when they get to push the elevator button. It won't take long, but after some serious study, you'll start to smile at the little things kids get excited about. They think dandelions are pretty, and when paired with wild violets, they become the most beautiful bouquet in the world. They love licking the leftover batter out of a bowl and putting ladybugs in a jar. They're giddy over the turkey wishbone and delighted by sparklers. They love walking barefoot in the grass and collecting seashells on the beach. It is undeniable that kids make a big deal out of little things; as far as I can tell, they seem to be having a pretty good time.

Maybe you could join me in trying to make a bit more of an effort to notice, and get excited by, the little things. Make an effort to foster within yourself a wonder and appreciation for the little things around you. I'm not promising that you'll suddenly regard Pizza Hut as a five-star restaurant, but I assure you it will do wonders in helping keep you young at heart. Because, as author Tim Hansel said, "Life is really fun, if we only give it a chance."

Delight in the Little Things

 Make it a point to carve out some time to watch a full sunrise. I know, you have to get up really early, but it's worth it. Take a good look at all of the colors and pay attention to the sounds of the world waking up.

 Take a friend to your favorite restaurant. Slow down and savor the food, and make note of all the little things that make it your favorite place to dine.

 Go to the nearest zoo. Spend some time *really* watching how the animals interact. Read the little signs by each exhibit. You'll be amazed at how perfectly suited each animal is to its particular habitat.

 Visit a state park and find a secluded area. Sit on a bench, a big rock, or the grass, and just be still. Tune out the distractions in your head and tune in to the calming sights and sounds around you. You might be surprised by what you notice.

Observe a child under the age of seven (perhaps a niece, nephew, or cousin, if you don't have one of your own).

Watch for what makes them tick and keep an eye out for the little things that delight them.

6 If you have a family, take a long weekend somewhere. Not necessarily someplace far or fancy, maybe even somewhere you've been many times before. When you're free from the distractions of new "things" to see and do, you can really focus on what's important—being together and having fun.

7 Make a mental list of three people you know who are worse off than you. Think of one nice little thing you could do for each of them, and do it. You'll gain a better appreciation of what you have, and by making someone else feel good, you'll feel good too.

8 Volunteer some time to help out a charitable organization, like Habitat For Humanity, The Make-A-Wish Foundation, or Big Brothers Big Sisters. You'll gain an almost immediate appreciation for the little things.

9 Rent the movie *City of Angels*. Pay close attention to the things Seth experiences with joy (and sometimes shock) that we routinely take for granted.

10 Go for a walk. When you're out of your normal environment, breathing some fresh air and getting the old heart rate up, it's a lot easier to take in some of the simple things in life that are missed on the commute to work.

Consider resurrecting a tradition that has unfortunately gone out of fashion in our busy culture: eating dinner with your family. All at once, all at the same time. Spend some time sharing highlights from the day. While seemingly trivial and insignificant, this little thing has tremendous power to bind a family together, creating memories that last forever.

Dream Big

*"Nurture your mind with great thoughts;
to believe in the heroic makes heroes."*

Benjamin Disraeli

What's the deal with Santa Claus?
I mean, how on earth did we buy into him when we were kids? Seriously. Somehow, back then, the whole concept of the big guy in the crimson suit was one-hundred percent feasible. Think about it. Take an old guy who never appears to age beyond, say, sixty-five, even though tradition has him old enough to make Yoda seem like a young buck. Somehow, he's able to

stop by every single kid's house on Christmas Eve. Every single one. Even if you take out the boys and girls who've been exceptionally bad (like John, who always makes fun of your shoes),

you still end up with a pretty staggering number of houses to crash. To be fair, I guess he *does* have the advantage of a magic sleigh pulled by eight flying reindeer (nine if Rudolph is on shift), which certainly eliminates any traffic snarls. But still, I haven't even touched on how he crams his jolly plump frame down your chimney (along with that new bike).

I thought I was a real Sherlock Holmes when I was younger and I asked my mom about the other kids in my class who didn't even *have* chimneys. Not to worry, she assured me, he gets into the house another way. Of course, I thought, he probably gets tips from the Tooth Fairy and the Easter Bunny. Somehow, it all makes perfect sense to kids. I'm just glad all these folks use their secret powers of entry for good and not evil, as I'm sure they'd make excellent burglars.

The peculiar thing is that for some reason, when we grow

up, we gradually lose the ability to see the magic in possibility. Now, before you put down this book and write me off as some wacko who advises people to believe in overweight elves and tooth-pilfering fairies, consider Orville and Wilbur Wright. They went around telling people that they'd very much like to fly. And they went so far as to start the process of creating a machine that would let them do so. I wonder what the townsfolk[1] said.

Riiiiight.

Do you get the feeling that a sense of overwhelming pride was not the first to cross their mother's mind? Can't you imagine the townsfolk saying, "How foolish, to be involved in such trivial pursuits!" (I'm not referring to the board game, as that hadn't been invented yet.) And yet the brothers persisted, determined to figure out a way to make science fit their lofty ambitions. They didn't let the naysayers convince them that it couldn't be done.

Yes, they failed many times, but not even the townsfolk would dispute their ultimate success. The last time I checked, there were about 50,000 of these harebrained, crazy flying machines operating in the United States every day. It amazes me how we take for granted such an impressive accomplishment that appeared incomprehensible less than 100 years ago. I think we all owe a debt of gratitude to the Wright brothers for daring to believe in such a ridiculous dream. And, speaking of travel, if not for Henry Ford's determination to live his dream, we might still be figuring out how to ride a better horse.

In 1943, IBM chairman Thomas Watson speculated that there to be a world market for maybe five computers. Decades later, a certifiably crazy young man named Steve Jobs envisioned that, someday, every person would have a computer in his or her home. "What on earth would a person do with a computer?" countered the critics. "What use would it serve?" With all due respect to Mr. Watson, there are people nowadays who have five computers—in their home.

In 1963, Martin Luther King, Jr. boldly dreamed that "little black boys and girls will be able to join hands with little white boys and girls and walk together as sisters and brothers" and that his own children would "one day live in a nation where they will not be judged by the color of their skin but by the content of their character." Many doubted the odds of his words ever coming true, but we have come a long way toward achieving his "impossible" dream.

I like motivational speaker Robert Kriegel's definition of a dream. He said, "A dream is an ideal involving a sense of possibilities rather than probabilities, of potential rather than limits. A dream is the wellspring of passion, giving us direction and pointing us to lofty heights. It is an expression of optimism, hope, and values lofty enough to capture the imagination and engage the spirit. Dreams grab us and move us. They are capable of lifting us to new heights and overcoming self-imposed limitations."

In one of his comedic routines, Jerry Seinfeld talks about young boys and their fascination with superheroes and comic books. He admits to the audience that to men, these are not merely stories—they're options. Little boys grow up considering the possibility of a career as a superhero. Wives all over the world might argue that those little boys are now men who sometimes think they've turned into such superheroes.

Growing up, I was no different. I admired them all, from Superman to Batman to Spiderman. I even quite fancied Iceman, as one-dimensional as he was. By day, I was Jason, mild-mannered son of Walt and Linda Kotecki, but I could turn into Superman at a moment's notice. (Okay, that's a bit of an exaggeration, especially when you're trying to change in a laundry closet with a burned-out light bulb.) Before long, I'd emerge wearing my authentic Superman Underoos® shirt, with my underpants pulled over my blue jeans, my trusty yellow blanket tied around my neck, and oversized red rubber rain boots loosely wobbling around my ankles. I imagined missions all around me, and a world where nothing was impossible.[2]

It's easy to cast aside a child's simplistic and naïve approach to the world, but let us never disregard an affinity for believing the impossible. If you ever think something is impossible, remember the bumblebee. According to the laws of aerodynamics and physics, it is supposed to be impossible for a bumblebee to fly. I guess the bumblebee never got the memo on that one.

> According to the laws of aerodynamics and physics, it is supposed to be impossible for a bumblebee to fly.

When I was in college, the mother of my favorite professor passed away. Upon returning from her funeral, he talked about what a full life she had lived (nearly a century's worth of years). He said that she had gone to school on dirt roads in a horse and buggy. Through the course of her life, she saw man travel to the moon, the invention of a moving picture box with

sound that we now call TV, cures for innumerable diseases, and the arrival of fax machines, cell phones, computers, and the Internet, all of which were either dubbed impossible or so "out there" that they hadn't even been previously imagined. It's hard to fathom what advances we'll see in the next 100 years, but I can assure you, somebody is already dreaming about the possibilities—probably a little kid somewhere. Neil Armstrong was one of those men who traveled to the moon and the first person to go for a stroll up there. He once said, "Ever since I was a little boy, I dreamed I would do something important in aviation." He, too, might have been considering a career as a flying superhero, but he's probably happy with how things ended up.

With all the evidence of the impossibilities becoming possible, why aren't more of us on the dream-big bandwagon? It's another side effect of Adultitis. In the process of "growing up," our minds became unconditioned to that way of thinking.

We're inundated by messages from people who say things like, "Quit spending your time chasing silly dreams," or "It's time to get serious," or "You're not good enough for that," or "Just who do you think you are?" We don't always realize how much of an impact those statements from others, and even our own thoughts and subconscious minds, have on the outcomes of our lives. Best-selling books have been written by scores of authors, well documenting the power of positive thinking. People have conquered long-held fears, financial troubles, and even illnesses with nothing more than positive thinking. If you don't believe me, get your hands on a copy of *The Power of Positive Thinking* by Norman Vincent Peale.[3] He gives countless examples of the importance of thinking positively and techniques on how to become more optimistic yourself.

Sometimes the only difference between winners and losers is the way they think about things. Thomas Edison (you know, that guy who invented the light bulb) only had about three months of formal schooling. He didn't look at failure as a negative thing. Upon being consoled by a friend for being unable to come up with a working model for a particular invention, he said, "I have not failed. I've just found 10,000 ways that won't work."

We encounter tons of pessimistic people every day (you might recognize them—they're the ones who call themselves realists). I have never seen negative, pessimistic thinking contribute to anything worthwhile. Think of the people you personally know who you consider to be successful. It could be in the realms of finance, family, career, or even faith. Those people probably have a generally optimistic outlook on life, and probably spend more time thinking positive thoughts than negative ones.

Think of it this way: imagine you have a sponge soaking in a bucket of muddy water. When you take out the sponge and squeeze it, would you expect clean water to come from it? Of course not. If our brains are soaking up muddy water (i.e., negative thoughts), we're not likely to see positive results.

I think another reason people shy away from the dreaming power of children is because of a thing called the "comfort zone." Believing in and chasing a dream takes a certain amount of energy and sacrifice. The rewards are fantastic, but sadly, many people are not willing to give up the comfort of their current lives to make the long-term commitment to see their dreams come true. It's certainly easier to sit on the sidelines and criticize others than to take up the challenge of a lofty dream. Barbara Grogan, founder of the $10 million company, Western Industrial Contractors, Inc., said in agreement, "The world is chock full of negative people...They have a thousand reasons why your dreams won't work, and they're ready to share them with you at the drop of a hat. Well, this sounds trite, but you just have to believe in yourself and in your ability to make your dreams come true."

Every once in a while, I find myself in a situation where the question is posed, "If you could be or do anything you wanted, what would that be?" It saddens me to see people who eagerly describe in detail what they'd love to be doing, while the reality of their situation is anything but. I have a difficult time answering questions like that, because if there were something else I'd really rather be doing that I'm not already doing (or not currently working toward), I would surely do something about it.

I was a very shy kid. Disturbingly shy. I was afraid of new situations, so much so that I avoided group sports and hated swimming lessons because I was too scared. I know my parents were concerned about me, and they often lamented about how many things I was missing out on. I wished they would just leave me alone.

But as I got a little older, I began to see they were right. In college I attended a retreat, and even though I had gone to a Catholic school, it was the first time I really started to "get" God. Through talks given by my peers and by people older than my parents, I began to see how real and relevant He really is. My faith started to grow, and even though I was still anxious about new situations, I began to rely on God's strength more

> "And the day came when the risk to remain tight in a bud was more painful than the risk it took to blossom."
>
> -Anaïs Nin

and more. Then one day, I stumbled across a quote by French writer Anaïs Nin, which stated, "And the day came when the risk to remain tight in a bud was more painful than the risk it took to blossom." Suddenly everything clicked. I was tired of missing out on life. The fear of regret for not having done something became greater than the anxiety of stepping out of my comfort zone. I decided that I didn't want to wake up someday regretting for all the opportunities I had missed because I was too frightened to try. That was something I needed to learn before I could take the first step toward my own dreams.

We all have obstacles in the way of our dreams. It is important to realize that these so-called obstacles are often not as immovable as we make them out to be. When people are questioned about why they're not pursuing their dreams, most of them usually respond with something like, "I have a family to support," or "I don't have the time for that," or "I'm no spring chicken," or "You have to know somebody to get involved in that," or "I'm not smart enough." Hogwash, I say. Those are negative thoughts, excuses we use to keep ourselves from trying. They may indeed be roadblocks to our dreams; but too often, we consciously or subconsciously give them too much power, allowing them to justify our decision to remain in our comfort zones. If being poor, having a family to support, lacking an education, or not being "connected" were legitimate dead-ends to success, then no one would have ever succeeded beyond them. History, however, gives us countless examples of people who overcame difficult obstacles, believed in their dreams, and changed the world.

You may know that Beethoven composed some of the most famous and beautiful musical masterpieces known to man. But did you know that he was deaf?

There are countless stories of people who have transcended formidable obstacles. For example, a young archer from Hungary lit up the 1952 Olympic games and won a gold medal by repeatedly splitting the target's bull's-eye. Tragically, he lost his right arm shortly after the games. But four years later, he returned to Olympic competition and claimed another gold—this time using his left hand.

Speaking of the Olympics, Wilma Rudolph became the first American woman to win three gold medals in track and field. She was born prematurely, and complications led to double pneumonia and scarlet fever. She spent the majority of her childhood in braces after a bout with polio left her with a crooked leg and a foot twisted inward.

At the age of 65, Harland "Colonel" Sanders was no spring chicken when he began franchising his Kentucky Fried Chicken business. And the first years were rough. Sanders said, "One of our biggest problems getting started was money. After we sold the restaurant at auction, I was getting $105 a month from social security. That paid for my gas and the travel needed to get the franchises started. Lots of nights I would sleep in the back of my car so I would have enough money to buy cookers the next day if someone took a franchise."

Thomas Mapother's parents divorced when he was twelve, and his father died of cancer shortly thereafter. Thomas had attended fourteen different schools by the time he was fourteen. Money was so tight that he gave his mother the earnings he received from his job as a paperboy. He struggled with shyness and dyslexia. He enjoyed wrestling, but suffered a knee injury that prevented him from pursuing it further. Hungry for something to do, he tried out for a school musical. A few plays later, he was hooked and decided to pursue his dream of becoming a great actor. Thomas didn't know anyone when he moved to New York at the age of 18, supporting himself by working as a busboy. With no connections, he endured many rejections, but finally, Thomas Mapother (you may know him as Tom Cruise), was cast in his first movie, *Endless Love*.

A. C. Giannini dreamed of starting a financial institution that served the little guy. Although he was a high school dropout, Giannini believed his concept could become a national bank. By making unheard-of automobile and appliance loans, his dream became a reality by the time of his death in 1949, and Bank of America was born.

When James Earl Jones was in elementary school, he had a horrible stuttering problem. It was so bad that he often communicated with people using written notes. Today he is celebrated for the richness of his voice. You may know James Earl Jones as the voice of Darth Vader from *Star Wars*.

If, in 1954, you happened to be born a black female, to poor, unwed teenage parents, your chances for success would not have been considered high. But Oprah Winfrey overcame many obstacles, including being raped by a cousin when she was nine years old, to become one of the most successful and influential people in the world.

There was once a young boy who was frequently beaten by his father and told he had no brains. Even a college advisor told him that, based on an aptitude test, he should pursue a job as an elevator repairperson. Instead, the boy pursued acting. While watching a fight between Muhammed Ali and Chuck Wepner, Sylvester Stallone was inspired to write the Academy Award winning movie, *Rocky*.

"Your dreams can come true. I'm living proof of it. I left home at seventeen and had nothing but rejections for twenty-five years. I wrote more than twenty-five screenplays, but I never gave up," states Michael Blake, author of *Dances With Wolves*.

Children believe in the impossible. There is no reason grown-ups shouldn't also. Take stock in the Queen's words to Alice in Lewis Carroll's *Through The Looking Glass*:

Alice laughed. "There's no use trying," she said. "One can't believe impossible things."

"I daresay you haven't had much practice," said the Queen. "When I was your age, I always did it for half an hour a day. Why, sometimes, I've believed as many as six impossible things before breakfast."

> ## "We ask ourselves, who am I to be brilliant, gorgeous, talented, fabulous? Actually, who are you not to be?"
> -Marianne Williamson

If you still doubt yourself and think these stories don't apply to you, consider the words of Marianne Williamson, as quoted in a speech by Nelson Mandela. "We ask ourselves, who am I to be brilliant, gorgeous, talented, fabulous? Actually, who are you not to be? You are a child of God. Your playing small does not serve the world. There is nothing enlightening about shrinking so that other people won't feel unsure around you. We were born to make manifest the glory of God that is within us. It is not just in some of us, it is in *everyone*."

Williamson and Mandela were right. God is a big and awesome God. He has planted unique dreams within us. He wants us to dream and do great things. If you give yourself half a chance to believe in yourself, to think positive thoughts, and to dream big, I guarantee you'll begin seeing new opportunities open up and possibilities that you've never imagined. Most of us want to make a difference in this life. In order to make an important difference, you need to be able to dream. As Robert Greenleaf, author of *Servant Leadership*, said, "Nothing much happens without a dream. For something really great to happen, it takes a really great dream."

We only need to model a child's ability to dream big to give ourselves an important start to seeing it come true. You see, a great advantage in being an adult is that we actually have the ability to take measured steps toward our dreams. Dreaming big is more than hopefully wishing for something to come true. Once you have your big dream in place, you can apply a time-tested process to systematically grow closer to your dream every day. First, write your dream down on paper. Secondly, convert that dream into specific goals. Then convert each of those goals into specific steps and each step into specific tasks. Next, assign a projected time or date to complete each task. Finally, spend time every day visioning and imagining your dream in great detail, using all of your senses, as if it has already come true. Perhaps you are skeptical, but this process helps to give you a realistic game plan to achieve your dream, making the impossible suddenly attainable.[4]

The question is: Are your dreams big enough? Author Glenn Van Ekeren tells the story of a college professor who prepared a test for his soon-to-be graduating seniors. The test questions were divided into three categories, and students were instructed to choose from only one. The first category was the hardest and worth fifty points. The second, which was easier, was worth forty points. The third, and simplest, was worth thirty points. Upon completion of the test, students who had chosen the fifty-point questions were given A's. The students who had chosen forty-point questions were given B's. Those who settled for the thirty-pointers were given C's. The students were frustrated with the grading of their papers and asked the professor what he was looking for. The professor leaned over the podium, smiled, and explained, "I wasn't testing your book knowledge. I was testing your aim."[5]

Children aim high. They grow up dreaming of careers as superheroes, ballerinas, professional baseball players, and President of the United States. They can spend an entire day in the backyard, digging in the sandbox, with the full intention of making it clear to China, or at the very least, uncovering a pile of old dinosaur bones. I challenge you to make an effort today to model a child's ability to dream big. Really big. Why waste your time dreaming little dreams? Dream big and you can accomplish things that you once thought were impossible. You'll make a profound difference in the lives of people around you. You'll have the fuel needed to achieve success beyond your wildest imagination. As musician Les Brown once said, "Shoot for the moon. Even if you miss, you'll land among the stars." I wonder what Neil Armstrong was shooting for.

If there were ever a time to dare,
to make a difference,
to embark on something worth doing,
it is now.
Not for any grand cause, necessarily—
but for something that tugs at your heart,
something that's your aspiration,
something that's your dream.

You owe it to yourself
to make your days here count.
Have fun.
Dig deep.
Stretch.
Dream big.

(Text from a 1991 Macintosh computer ad)

Dream Big

1 If you could do anything with your life, and money, age, family background, and education were not obstacles, what would you do? Even if you don't believe it could ever happen, write it down on paper. There is magic in writing things down.

2 Think of some people you really admire, especially those who are doing something similar to what you'd like to do. Find and read biographies about these people for inspiration. You may be surprised that they had bigger obstacles to overcome than you.

3 When you have your dream written down, take a few moments every day, if you can, and imagine in great detail a day when you have achieved your dream. Be as specific as you can with your thoughts. Include all of your senses in your vision.

4 Follow the process of breaking down your dream into goals, steps and tasks. Start this week working toward task number one. I recommend the book, *The Success Principles,* by Jack Canfield, co-author of the *Chicken*

Soup for the Soul series. It provides 64 specific principles to help you chart your way to success.

5 Buy or borrow *The Power of Positive Thinking* by Norman Vincent Peale to learn more about how to think your way to success.

6 I enjoy dreaming with a group of friends. Meet regularly with your closest friends and share with each other what you'd like to be doing ten years from now. Have fun. Don't let fear or negative thoughts prevent you from stretching your imagination.

7 Is your dream impossible? Remember the bumblebee. Assuredly, you have some major obstacles in your path, but you have the power within you to think of ways around them. Work on a list of some ways around your obstacles. If you're having trouble, ask a friend (someone whom you consider to be a positive thinker) for ideas.

8 Spend more time with people who are "dream makers," rather than "dream breakers." The positive energy of a dream maker is contagious, and will provide you with the encouragement you need on your way to your dream.

9 We only have so much time given to us. If you are not currently chasing a dream, consider this: How will you feel twenty or thirty years from now, knowing you didn't at least give it a try?

10 Make a list of ten things that didn't exist 100 (or even 50) years ago. Those ten things exist because somebody believed in the power of possibility. Keep your list handy to remind you that something that seems impossible today can be your reality tomorrow.

11 Write down Marianne Williamson's quote mentioned earlier in this chapter and refer to it often. Keep in mind that most people who have risen to high levels of success started out from very humble beginnings.

Get Curious

"I think, at a child's birth, if a mother could ask a fairy godmother to endow it with the most useful gift, that gift would be curiosity."

Eleanor Roosevelt

It was a nightly routine: a childlike version of *Jeopardy!* in which my dad was always the contestant. My brother Dan played the role of host Alex Trebek.

We shared a bedroom growing up (no, not Alex and I, Dan and I). We each had our own bed, mine outfitted with Star Wars sheets, Dan's with a nice *Dukes of Hazzard* print. Snugly tucked under the covers, we waited to hear the water start running in the sink of the upstairs bathroom. It was Dad, patiently waiting for the water to get cold so he could bring us an icy glass to sip right before lights-out. He'd come in a few minutes later, proudly claiming that this was the coldest glass of water ever. He'd sit on the edge of the bed and wait for us to finish our drinks. These moments often provided one more opportunity to reflect on the day and bring up anything that was on our minds. It didn't take long for the first question to be launched.

"Dad, how do they make beer?"

The questions always came from my brother, a new one every night.

"What makes people grow?"

I'd usually lie in bed and listen as Dad fielded the evening's question, always in a confident manner. (If I had an opportunity to check the tape and review his answers, I have a sneaky feeling that they wouldn't quite have matched up with *Encyclopedia Britannica*.)

"Why did they decide to make money green?"

Sometimes I was embarrassed for my brother, but I always stayed alert enough to hear the answer. Dad faithfully stayed long enough to answer the question, fully and thoughtfully, before turning out the lights. Those episodes say a lot about the patience of a father who is expected to know everything (aren't they all?), but also quite a bit about the natural curiosity of my brother and children in general.

Anyone with a three-year-old will tell you that her favorite word is *why*. Parents do the best they can to deal with the onslaught of curiosity, but apparently, there IS a limit to just

how many "why" questions one human being can handle. By the time the kids become teenagers, all parents can seem to muster is, "Because I said so."

Questions come easily for children, and curiosity is found in abundance. Certainly that makes sense, because, to a child, everything is new and undiscovered, begging to be explored. "Curiosity in children is but an appetite for knowledge," said John Locke, a seventeenth-century British philosopher. "One great reason why children abandon themselves wholly to silly pursuits and trifle away their time insipidly is because they find their curiosity balked, and their inquiries neglected."

It seems that the taller we get, the shorter our range of curiosity becomes. It's hard to say why exactly, especially because even after one attains a masters degree, or even a doctorate, there is no shortage of knowledge yet to be attained. In this information age, we could live to be a thousand and probably still not learn everything there is to learn.

I happen to be an introvert and particularly hate small talk. Why waste time on idle chitchat when we could be talking about more important things? Or at least more interesting things. I seem to be in a minority in that I'm always asking questions of people, especially those involved in a field with which I'm completely unfamiliar. I'm not going to pretend that I know what someone's talking about if I really don't. I've found that by humbling yourself and admitting you're not quite familiar with someone's occupation or particular interest, you help make that person feel important and give her the opportunity to talk about herself. And people love to talk about themselves. It boggles my mind why more people don't try this approach. Besides getting the other person to think more favorably of you because you've taken a sincere interest, you also stand a good chance of learning something new and interesting. I once heard Jack Canfield tell a story about a discussion he had with a friend, in which he asked her not only where she wanted to be in three years, but what obstacles she would have to overcome and what opportunities she would have to take advantage of in order to get there. Jack's friend grew more and more excited as she talked about her dreams. Now, he had barely said a word the whole evening, but at the end of their night together, she thanked him for his insight and commented that it had been the best conversation they ever had. All because he asked a few sincere questions and really listened.

Perhaps we're so concerned about fitting in that we don't

want to rock the boat by asking questions, or maybe even more likely, we don't want to appear foolish in front of others by admitting that we might not know something. It's hard to dispute the fact that natural curiosity appears to wane as we grow up. I suppose that schools themselves could share the blame as well. Albert Einstein himself said, "It is, in fact, nothing short of a miracle that the modern methods of instruction have not yet entirely strangled the holy curiosity of inquiry."

In any case, by stifling our natural curiosity, we really miss out on a lot. Not only do we miss the opportunity to broaden our range of knowledge so we can make a respectable showing should we ever land on *Jeopardy!*, but we may also miss an opportunity to improve our lives, or even to change the world. That's right, change the world. Far-fetched?

Please consider Benjamin Franklin. Mr. Franklin was quite a curious individual, eager to ask questions, embark on grand adventures and try new things. He loved to read. When he was sixteen, he began eating only vegetables in order to cut his food costs so that he could buy more books. When he was 18, he went to London to study the latest developments in printing. Upon his return to America, he launched the first paper to use political cartoons (the *Pennsylvania Gazette*). At the age of 26, he published the first edition of his *Poor Richard's Almanac*.

> By stifling our natural curiosity, we may miss an opportunity to change the world.

In his thirties, Franklin got more involved in civic affairs, and his curiosity led him to begin making scientific observations. He studied the weather, and predicted that a storm's course could be plotted. It was he who introduced the maxim, "An apple a day keeps the doctor away," when one of his studies concluded that a diet including apples helped maintain healthy gums and skin.

As Franklin grew older, his childlike curiosity did not subside. He became interested in electricity after seeing demonstrations about electric charges. He performed many experiments, including one that involved a key and a kite. He believed that electricity came from the clouds, and he invented the lightning rod, which attracted electricity and helped protect people's homes. He set up America's first fire insurance company. He coined the terms "battery," "conductor," "positive and negative charge," and "electrician."

Franklin wore glasses, and when he was in his forties, he developed the need of another pair for reading. He split the lenses of each pair, with the top lens to be used for seeing distances, and the bottom for reading, so he wouldn't have to constantly be changing his glasses. These were the first bifocals. He also invented the Franklin stove and the catheter. And he was the first to come up with the proposal for Daylight Saving Time.

Benjamin Franklin's life was one of great influence, as a publisher, scientist, and politician. Remarkably, he had no formal education in the sciences. He gained insights and ideas from conversations he had with scientists, and yet relied predominantly on his own powerful observations and insatiable curiosity. It is an amazing testament to see the power of a life fueled with such an undiluted childlike curiosity. And it would be pretty hard to argue that he didn't change the world with that curiosity.

Children come into the world with fresh eyes. Everything they observe is new. I think children spend most of their time in their early years just observing. That's probably due partially to the fact that everything is so new, but also, I would guess, because there's not much else to do when you log so many hours uncomfortably strapped into a high chair or car seat. A child's observation of parents, siblings, and society at large, leads to many important discoveries and contributes greatly to that child's development. But who says that this has to end in adulthood? As Mr. Franklin's life shows us, the power of curious observation can do wonders for anybody—car seat not included.

An open, observant mind, one receptive to the magic of curiosity, can generate some very good (and profitable) ideas. For instance, Leo Gerstenzang saw his wife awkwardly trying to clean her baby's ears with toothpicks and cotton, and the idea for Q-Tips® was born. Let's all be grateful for that one. Who wants to see toothpicks being jammed into the ears of little babies?

Roy Speer and Lowell Paxson observed three things about people's lifestyles: (1) People like to shop; (2) people like to watch TV; and (3) people like to do both of these things any-time they wish. Speer and Paxson made hundreds of millions of dollars by capitalizing on those observations and creating the Home Shopping Network, a 24-hour-a-day TV shopping channel.

King C. Gillette was looking for an idea for a throwaway product to market. Upon finding his razor dull, he thought of the safety razor with disposable blades. Reportedly, it's the best a man can get.

While in India, a man named Will Parish curiously observed how a dinner he ate was heated with flaming cow dung. Appetizing, I know. The burning cow pie led Parish to create National Energy Associates, which burns 900 tons of manure a day, producing enough megawatts to light 20,000 American homes. *Fortune* magazine dubbed him the world's true "entre-manure."

The ability to look at life from the ever-questioning mindset of a child can help lead to opportunities for great improvement. There was one fellow you've undoubtedly heard of who looked at a situation around him and wondered if things might be done better. He often took his young family to traveling carnivals. He became disgusted with the shoddy equipment, rude workers, and dirty environment that seemed to be synonymous with the carnival. Vulgarity and grime were common, sanitation was not a priority, and most of these amusement parks were not exactly family-friendly. He envisioned the concept of a family-oriented amusement park that was well-maintained, clean, and staffed with friendly workers. It was an idea that seems to make common sense now, but at the time, the man had a heck of a time convincing investors to

put up the money he needed for this family utopia. Of course, the man's name was Walt Disney and he ended up calling his vision "Disneyland."

I think what these examples show is how important it is to keep your eyes open, no matter how old you are. There is much to be gained via the art of observation. While we naturally seem to "outgrow" the inquisitiveness that can make a four-year-old pick up a dead bird found on the side of the road and stick it in his pocket, it's important to remember that curiosity is really a state of mind, an attitude. Fortunately, that's something available to everyone, even those over 36 inches tall.

My childhood home was right next to a ravine. A grouping of ancient trees wrapped around a skinny stream; it was a treasure chest of boyhood wonder. Countless afternoons were spent exploring the land as if it were a lost Amazon jungle. Mossy rocks, decaying leaves, and scurrying creepy-crawly things whispered of mysteries great and small. I'd carefully collect the tools of all great explorers: a flashlight, a compass, a *Star Wars* Thermos® filled with pink lemonade, and a butter

dish to hold collected samples to be examined back at the lab. I'd spend hours in that ravine. I remember being amazed when I'd find an old, rusty soda can, emblazoned with a design and brand name I didn't recognize. I would speculate how many centuries old it was, as if I had just uncovered an ancient civilization. If I were to visit the ravine today, I'm sure I'd be utterly underwhelmed, probably surprised at how much it had "shrunk." I'd be scratching my head as to how anyone could find more than a half an hour of amusement there. I'm certain that you can recall many similar experiences from your own childhood—moments and places that once seemed extraordinary, that now seem so much less so.

> Curiosity is an attitude, a state of mind. It is not limited to the young, but it is they who have it truly mastered.

And so it is. The fact is that *we* have changed, not the place. Curiosity is an attitude, a state of mind. And it can become a conscious decision. Our curiosity is waiting to be unleashed. There is no shortage of good opportunities available to us, from holding a newborn to marveling at the patterns of a snowflake. Curiosity is not limited to the young, but it is they who have it truly mastered.

I think one of the most important words in the vocabulary of anyone who wants to be successful is the same word that three-year-olds use every day: *Why.*

Why *is vanilla ice cream white when vanilla extract is brown?*

Why *do companies offer you "free gifts?" Since when has a gift NOT been free?*

Why *is it good to score under par in golf but it's bad to be "under par" in anything else?*

Why *does a round pizza come in a square box?*

Why *can't we sneeze with our eyes open?*

Why *is there not a Channel 1 on TV?*

Why *do people point to their wrist when asking for the time, but don't point to their crotch when they ask where the bathroom is?*

Why *do old men have hair in their ears?*

Why *would Superman want to leap over the tallest building in a single bound when he can fly?*

And **why** *did Superman wear his briefs on the outside of his tights?*[1]

I'm sure you have your own laundry list of "why" questions. It's very simple, but asking "why" can lead to useful solutions to seemingly unsolvable problems. And those solutions can come from the unlikeliest of places. A story I once heard about The El Cortez Hotel in San Diego offers one example. The management of the upscale hotel decided that the current elevator was not cutting the mustard. It was not able to efficiently transport the guests between their rooms and the lobby. So they decided to bring in a team of capable architects and engineers to solve the problem. The solution proposed by the team of experienced builders was to cut a hole in each floor from the basement all the way to the top of the hotel in order to install a new elevator.

A janitor overheard the experts discussing their plan. "What are you up to?" he asked.

The team explained their idea. The janitor shook his head. "That's going to make quite a mess. There will be a lot of debris and plaster and dust."

Undaunted, the architects and engineers explained that they were planning to have the hotel closed while the project was underway. The janitor spoke up again. "That will lose the hotel a lot of money. And there will be many people who will be out of work until the project is completed."

Exasperated, one of the experts said, "Well, do you have a better idea?"

The janitor thoughtfully leaned on his mop and pondered the challenge. "Why don't you build the elevator on the outside of the hotel?"

The team of engineers looked at each other and responded, "Hmm...that's never been done before. Let's do it!" And, with that, the El Cortez Hotel became the birthplace of a popular architectural first, making it even more noteworthy and undoubtedly bringing in more revenue for the hotel owners.

There have been countless businesses that have crumbled and disappeared primarily because people within the organization forgot to ask "why?" A company might be in trouble when the answer to any "why" question is "Because we've always done it that way." Likewise, many opportunities have opened up and businesses been built thanks to individuals who have heard, "We've always done it this way," and asked, "Why?"

Only men should be allowed to vote... Why?

The only market for computers will be very large corporations... Why?

We all concur that the world is flat... Why?

When it comes to my own company, I've tried to make a concerted effort to make sure everyone is comfortable with asking questions about our plans, procedures, or policies. As of this writing, we've only been in business for about five years, and already there are things we do that are outdated. For instance, our first greeting card offerings were fairly popular with buyers, but we felt they weren't selling as well as they could be. That led us to ask, "Why is that?" We came to discover that it was primarily because they were blank on the inside (even though a full message was usually on the front). As we investigated further, we found that most people pick up a card and open it, expecting something to be on the inside. After stumbling upon something that now seemed fairly obvious, we were led to the next "why?" We wondered why in the heck we ever designed the cards this way in the first place, even though we intuitively knew that most people buy cards with a sentiment on the inside. We ultimately learned that it was not because we were a bunch of ignorant knuckleheads, but rather because when we originally developed the first card line, we couldn't afford the double-sided printing. It was either print cards with the messages on the front, or no cards at all. Since then, our budget has expanded and we've developed a more

---

traditional line, but our old line continues to be popular with people who like to add their own personal touch inside.[2] The original reason for what we did was sound, but without asking why, we might not have been able to move forward successfully.

Now that's a fairly simple example, but I know that as our business grows, there are likely to be many things we do out of habit (which started for very honorable and sensible reasons) that are now extremely inefficient. When you're so close to the situation, it's hard to notice the problems, let alone think to ask why. But at every staff meeting, I elect one person to serve as the "Why Guy" or "Why Gal." That person has a handful of cards emblazoned with the word "Why?" that he or she is encouraged to play over the course of the meeting. The "Why Person" asks a question, and the person who is talking has to explain the who, why, where, when, or what. It's done in a very respectful way.

A friend of mine from England helped out as a consultant during the early days of our company. Jacqui was quite fond of using the word "why," often being quite forward when she asked it. To be honest, it really took us aback at first. But she explained that in England, people ask "why" all the time. It's not to challenge an individual or express doubt, but rather to show a sincere desire to understand the other person more fully. She shared her experience of how Americans tend to be quite defensive to her style. Jacqui helped us to understand the importance of the word "why."[3]

The sheer act of *not* asking "why" can actually be quite hazardous to one's health. Adolf Hitler was quoted as saying,

----

"What luck for rulers that men do not think." Through the ages, many millions of people have been victimized by evil men simply because they didn't take the time to ask "why?"

Being curious and asking plenty of questions helps you become wiser and more knowledgeable, uncover opportunities to solve unsolvable problems, and open doors to improve the financial standing of your family, your friends, or your business.

I shall close with another thought from my white-haired friend Einstein, who was quite passionate about this subject of curiosity. He said, "The important thing is not to stop questioning. Curiosity has its own reason for existing. One cannot help but be in awe when he contemplates the mysteries of eternity, of life, of the marvelous structure of reality. It is enough if one tries merely to comprehend a little of this mystery every day. Never lose a holy curiosity."[4]

I guess even a genius can embrace a childlike spirit. I wonder if he knew how they made beer.

Get Curious

1 The next time you're in a conversation with someone you don't know very well, skip the small talk and exhibit a sincere interest in what he does. Don't be afraid to ask for clarification if you don't understand. Once he knows you're sincere, he'll appreciate your interest and happily explain further. Plus, you may learn something.

2 Educational shows have come a long way. The Discovery Channel, History Channel, Animal Planet, and Food Network are just a few of the programming stations on television that offer an abundance of interesting shows on a variety of topics. Check your TV listings for some programs that might pique your curiosity.

3 Go to a bookstore and lose yourself in a section you wouldn't normally frequent. Charles Schulz, the creator of the comic strip *Peanuts*, was a big proponent of the idea that you can gain some great insights by exposing yourself to something outside your normal sphere of influence.

4 Are you curious about something in particular? Read a book, take a class, or explore the Internet for more on your subject of interest. Being curious is a great way to teach yourself anything.

5 Write the word "Why?" in big, bold letters on a note card. Carry it around with you as a reminder to ask yourself that question on a regular basis. "Why do I do the laundry at this time?" "Why do we handle customer complaints this way?" "Why don't I assign someone else to this task?"

6 Visit a nearby museum. If they have one of those self-guided audio tours, take advantage of it. It can be a great way to get an overview of some of the more interesting things the museum has to offer.

7 Think about your job. Are you stuck, bored, or burned out? Can you find other people who have a similar job and who have taken a different approach? What have they done differently? Why? Interview them, or read about them. Perhaps some of their ideas will spark an exciting new direction for you.

8 Make it a personal mission to learn something new every day. Read lots of books. It is well known that leaders are readers. That's why mansions always have libraries in them.

9 Don't be afraid to ask questions. A greater understanding of a subject can lead to new insights and real breakthroughs. My dad is good at asking questions. When I was a freelance artist, many opportunities were opened up for me because he asked probing questions to people he encountered in his job. So, be it at work, in class, or at the supermarket, make it a point to ask questions.

10 It's always good to expose yourself to new environments. Constantly being around people who live as you do and have beliefs exactly like yours is a sure way to kill off curiosity. Visit a new country, city, or restaurant.

11 Check out www.howthingswork.com. They have a ton of fascinating but brief articles on curiosity-filled topics, like "How Lock Picking Works" and "How Hair Dryers Work." They also have some neat books for excellent bathroom reading.

Live Passionately

*"Only passions, great passions, can elevate
the soul to great things."*

Denis Diderot

Nein Nunb. Bossk. Grand Moff Tarkin.

Any idea what I'm referring to? Most likely not, I would imagine. Only people who grew up during the height of the *Star Wars* phenomenon in the late seventies and early eighties might be able to make a guess. But even then, only those with a rabid fascination for the science fiction series would be able to say with certainty that Nein Nunb was Lando Calrissian's co-pilot in the mission to destroy the Death Star, Bossk was one of the most feared bounty hunters in the galaxy, and Grand Moff Tarkin was an Imperial Governor and mastermind of the original Death Star. Now there's some perfectly useless trivia for you.

As a young boy with a wild imagination, the *Star Wars* movies fascinated me. There was little I was more passionate about. I had most of the original ships and action figures. My loving parents sacrificed many hours searching countless racks of *Star Wars* figures in toy stores across the Midwest in hopes of finding one I didn't have. A

The peculiar thing about children is that they can turn any ordinary occurrence into a cause for great celebration.

kotecki

task easier said than done, you should know. And you *would* know if you ever tried to look through a long row of blister packs jammed on a not-long-enough peg hook in a toy store. By the time you try to get a look at the fourth package, the first one falls off the hook, and before long, you're left with a pile of unwanted action figures on the floor.

Clean up in aisle five.

I grew up knowing just about every line of dialogue from the movies, I memorized all of the names of the characters (even the minor ones, as you've seen), and admired the vision and creativity of George Lucas, the creator of *Star Wars*. I had

Star Wars birthday cakes, a *Star Wars* lunchbox, a *Star Wars* bank, *Star Wars* coloring books, and ate *Star Wars* cereal. I went to sleep in a bed outfitted with *Star Wars* sheets while wearing *Star Wars* pajamas and dreaming little *Star Wars* dreams. As I said, there was little I was more passionate about.

But kids are that way. It's easy for them to get passionate about things. *Star Wars* has experienced a resurgence with the recent releases of the "prequels," and many youngsters a third of my age are getting into it. But beyond even *Star Wars*, just about every kid

can name a favorite character from this group: Mickey Mouse, Big Bird, Elmo, Superman, Barney, Winnie The Pooh, Cinderella, Bugs Bunny.

My wife's cousin Jacob was really passionate about cowboys when he was younger. Everything was about cowboys. He had toy guns, cowboy action figures, and even a full cowboy outfit.

Through my involvement with The Make-A-Wish Foundation®, I met a boy named Kyle who had an extreme passion for Buzz Lightyear from the Pixar movie, *Toy Story*. I knew Buzz was a rambunctious spaceman character voiced by Tim Allen, but before I met Kyle, I had no idea they made so many different versions of Buzz Lightyear—big Buzz, little Buzz, Buzz with a silver suit, Buzz with a purple suit, Buzz that talks, Buzz that moves... and on and on. I wonder if they make one that cuts the grass for you.

One dictionary definition of "passion" describes it as "great enthusiasm." I suppose that would describe my affinity for *Star Wars*. But I'm not even limiting this idea of childlike passion to licensed characters and marketing hoopla. The dictionary also describes the word as meaning "a powerful feeling," with synonyms including enthusiasm, fervor, fire, and zeal. One of my nephews is a real bear in the morning. Besides a raging case of bed head, he has very little of anything percolating when he first wakes up, but once he gets going, there is very little he does without enthusiasm, fervor, fire, and zeal.

Kids tackle most activities they encounter with passionate and reckless abandon. Think about a youngster unwrapping a large present on his birthday. The shredded paper left in the aftermath is proof that the activity was not lacking fervor. What about when a girl gets to run free in a park with a tremendous climbing area? Shortness of breath and skinned knees don't happen to someone without at least a *little* fire. And have you seen a child attack a chocolate ice cream cone on a summer day? I submit that the hopelessly stained shirt is undoubtedly owned by someone with a healthy helping of zeal.

It's hard to imagine many situations that children don't bring passion to. Heck, they even avoid eating broccoli with high levels of passion. Yet what seems so easy to see in children is often very hard to find in adults—especially the ones infected with Adultitis. A typical morning commute will provide plenty of examples of passionless people. Our passions have been buried in an avalanche of routine and mundane chores. We get bored with life, most of which is dictated by someone other than ourselves.

Passion and enthusiasm can make a difference in even the littlest matters. We all have tasks in life that give us little choice about whether they can be done or not. Things we don't particularly like. But you can use a bit of passion to help bring some enjoyment even to those activities. When my brothers and I were young, my mother often instructed us to "go clean the playroom." Naturally, we had more fun playing in the playroom than cleaning it, and she usually got really serious about it when it became especially difficult to see the floor. So, as we trudged down the steps to "do the nasty," we made a little competition out of it. We sang a song we made up and tried to see how fast we could clean up the room. I'm sure it did not deliver the most orderly of results, but the toys were put away, the floor was visible, and we were free to do more enjoyable things—like more playing.[1]

"Fires can't be made with dead embers," says psychologist James Mark Baldwin. "Nor can enthusiasm be stirred by spiritless men. Enthusiasm in our daily work lightens efforts and turns every labor into pleasant tasks." So when faced with the unenjoyable task of mowing the lawn or cleaning the bathroom, why not make a tape or CD of some of your favorite energizing songs to listen to? In the comfort of your own bathroom, you can even feel free to lip-sync the lyrics without the neighbors giving strange looks. As you cut the grass, you

----

might play a little game with yourself to see how perfectly even you can cut the rows, or imagine you're mowing the outfield for your favorite team—the very team whose game you'll be able to watch as soon as you've finished the job.

In the bigger picture, our dwindling supply of passion is a curious issue. It's a phenomenon that spans continents. A European artist once drew a cartoon with two panels. The first one showed a group of small children entering a subway tunnel. They exhibited the perfect expression of enthusiasm and joy—smiling, laughing, playfully tossing their hats in the air. The second panel showed a crowd of emotionless adults, drudging out of the tunnel wearing dull, zombie-like expressions. There was no caption, but none was really necessary.

Is your morning Danish served with a side of dread and dullness? Or do you get out of bed every day excited about what the day will bring? Kids do. They're eagerly up at the crack of dawn to tackle the new day with energy and enthusiasm (and not in the least concerned with wasting any time fixing the bed head or extinguishing morning breath, I might add). I agree with Holiday Inn® founder Kemmons Wilson, Sr., who said, "If you don't have enthusiasm, you don't have anything."

Except maybe an advanced case of Adultitis.

> Do you get out of bed every day excited about what the day will bring? Or is your morning Danish served with a side of dread and dullness?

The question is plain. What happens as we grow up that causes us to live lives that are so stale and tedious? Why don't we spend more time on things we're truly passionate about? Why are so many of us stuck in unfulfilling careers? Are we waiting for some sort of permission? If so, I give you permission, right now.

Spend more time on things you're passionate about. Maybe it's just me, but kids sure do make it look fun.

Start with your hobbies or interests. Are you spending time doing stuff you really love, whether it's gardening, scrapbooking, cooking, drawing, or helping out with the decorations at church? You and your loved ones will benefit greatly if you can figure out a way to squeeze in a little more time for your hobbies.

But why stop at the hobbies, I say. Take a look at your career, if you have one. Are you spending the bulk of your waking hours on something you're passionate about? If so, great! If not... why not? Did you know that people stuck in unfulfilling career paths often experience headaches, stomachaches, loss of appetite, high blood pressure, lack of sleep, and even depression? Yikes. If you ask me, those are pretty sure signs that your body is trying to tell you something.

Too many of us are stuck in jobs that we not only lack passion for, but that we actually HATE. Unfortunately, Charles Lamb, essayist and children's book author, was onto something when he said, "Our spirits grow grey before our hairs." Are you one of those people who thinks it's impossible to do something you're passionate about AND make a living at it? Guess again. Time and time again, countless people have proved the axiom to be true: Do what you love and the money will follow. I am lucky to have in my own life several examples of people who have made a career out of what they're passionate about. If you look hard enough, I'm sure you'll find that you know some, too.

My friend Sue is a sign language interpreter. At a concert one evening, I had the opportunity to witness her in action. There were times when I found it hard to decide whether to focus my attention on the musical performers or on Sue. She not only had a way of interpreting the lyrics sung into hand gestures, but she somehow captured the essence and feeling of the music as well. She was so graceful and expressive; it was really amazing. And it's hard to explain unless you've seen it. Watching her, I was struck with how she had taken this normally quite functional task of interpretation and turned it into an art form. It was one of the most beautiful things I've seen in a long while. I know that signing is a deep passion for Sue, and it radiates from her when she does it. It started out very simply as she learned the skill from her boyfriend. It became a thrilling volunteer opportunity. And now she's making a good living doing it. It made me think, as I am prone to do from time to time, that we all have

> Are you one of those people who think it's impossible to do something you're passionate about AND make a living at it? Guess again.

some sort of passion, a piece of God, that is begging to be let out. It's bouncing around in there, waiting for our permission to just release it. When we do, it's a beautiful thing; it's like a whisper from God to the world. Sue loves interpreting. It's her passion.

My brother-in-law Gene is a financial advisor. He's an expert on stocks and bonds and mutual funds. But what makes him really successful in a crowded field of pushy stock salesmen and wannabes is his deep-seated passion for helping people. You can see it in his eyes when he talks about how he was able to help an elderly couple have a nicer retirement than they anticipated, or how he helped a young couple set up an investment plan that would give them a solid foundation and financial freedom down the road. Gene regularly sends personal notes to all of his clients and often attends the wakes and funerals of people he served. People feel comfortable with Gene and refer others to him, because he's sincere and passionate about what he does. He's the type of person who can't imagine ever completely retiring because he's having such a ball.

Artist Edward B. Butler has some words of wisdom along these lines. He said, "Every man is enthusiastic at times. One man has enthusiasm for 30 minutes; another man has it for 30 days; but it is the man who has it for 30 years who makes a success in life."

It all makes sense, doesn't it? The benefits are easy to see. When you're doing what you love, you're more likely to put in the extra hours and make the sacrifices that are needed to be successful. In the long run, you'll be more productive because you're interested in the work at hand. And the time you spend "working" won't seem like work at all because you're actually enjoying yourself. Enthusiasm makes things more fun.

Don't think for a second that you are excluded from being able to really embrace that which you are passionate about. Every day, people bury their passions, thinking that because they have physical limitations, don't have an education, or don't have time because they are busy supporting their family, they are doomed to a passionless existence. Everyone has obstacles that stand in the way, but passion is the number one key to success. If what you want to do requires education, your passion will lead you to it. Passion will also help you through the tough times, the hard work, and the sacrifice. The decision is ultimately yours on whether you follow your passion or remain right in your rut. (As Ellen Glasglow said, "The only difference between a rut and a grave…is in their dimensions.") No book could cover all of the people who embraced their passions and persevered with enthusiasm in spite of their disadvantages.

There was one young boy who grew up in Tennessee with a burning passion for music. It consumed him, and there was nothing he was more enthusiastic about. His disadvantaged childhood was not filled with encouragement and opportunity, however. He was able to get ahold of a battered and used guitar, but lacked any knowledge of how to play it. One day, his cousin, a country music singer, stopped by for a visit and helped the eager youngster tune his battered instrument and showed him how to play a few simple chords. It was all the young boy would need to make his passion even more resolute. Not many years later, the young musician would spin his passion into a career and steal the hearts of millions of people all over the world. It was the pursuit of passion despite unimpressive beginnings that helped Elvis Presley become successful.[2]

It is often said that you don't choose your passion, but rather that your passion chooses you. I think we were all born with something inside of us that really excites us, something that we are very enthusiastic about. Indeed, the word enthusiasm comes from the Greek roots "en" and "theos," meaning "God within." It's a fire within you. On her web site, career coach Leslie Martin says, "Passion is that divine spark that fuels direction. It isn't necessarily seen, but you know it when you experience it. You feel it at a deep level. And that desire to do something meaningful is in the heart of every person."

Are you unsure what your true passion is? Think about what things come easily to you or what activities make you feel most alive. Those can be strong indicators. Your passion is kind of like a kid brother. It follows you around wherever you go, pestering you all the while, not content until you stop and spend some time with it.

If you can't figure out what exactly your passion might be, sometimes it helps to look back at your childhood, the time when passion seemed easier to come by. Think for a moment about what you wanted to be when you grew up. That can often provide you with clues about the passions you were born with.

Now don't get ahead of me here. Just because you wanted to be an astronaut when you were five doesn't mean you should start packing your bags for the nearest NASA space camp. Think about what you wanted to be when you "grew up" and take a deeper look into the reason *why* you wanted to become that. If you wanted to be an astronaut, why? Was it because you liked science, or discovering new things? If so, are you currently in a field or pursuing a career involving science, or one that allows you to experiment and try new things? If your dream was to become the President of the United States, was it because you wanted to lead people, or inspire people, or have people respect you? Perhaps you should be developing your leadership skills and looking for opportunities that allow you to lead and inspire people.

I was usually contemplating two primary career choices when I was a kid. Like George Lucas, I wanted to be a movie producer. I also wanted to be a superhero. Something on the level of a Superman or Batman or Spiderman. Now, I don't have any big-budget releases planned for the summer, and I don't go around wearing a cape and multi-colored, close-fitting bodysuits (be very, very thankful for that). But you may be surprised to find that I am actually fulfilling the essence of those pie-in-the-sky professions. The reason I wanted to be like George Lucas was not necessarily because I had a deep desire to make movies. I was intrigued by how he created such great stories, characters and imaginary worlds. He entertained people. As a cartoonist, I too find myself ever in the midst of imagining new storylines, developing my characters, and trying to entertain my audience.

And while x-ray vision and bulletproof skin would be cool traits to possess, the biggest reason I wanted to be a superhero was to help people, especially those who couldn't help themselves. I wanted to make a difference. Through my comic strip, visits to schools and organizations, and my company's contri-

Career Choices From Childhood: Veterinarian.

butions to charities that help children all over the world, I think I'm doing a pretty good job of being a hero in my own unique way. By the way, aspiring to superhero status is not the only dream job that speaks of a hidden desire to make a difference by helping others. Pay attention, those of you who dreamed of becoming a firefighter, teacher, cowboy, or veterinarian! But remember, we cannot truly fulfill our purpose in life until we pinpoint our passion.[3]

When it comes down to it, most people want to look back on their lives with the peaceful confidence that they made some sort of a difference during the time they inhabited this little blue marble known as Earth. The truth is that you have to care very deeply about something in order to make a difference. The Mel Gibson film *Braveheart* portrayed the life of Sir William Wallace, who stood for the freedom of Scotland from England against remarkable odds. He was ultimately executed at the hands of the English, but his overwhelming passion inspired his fellow countrymen to gain their independence. Indeed, history positively remembers the likes of Wallace, Martin Luther King, Jr., Mother Teresa, Gandhi, and others—people with remarkable passion.

Sometimes passion for something worthwhile is born from tragedy. The magazine *Driven* recounts the story of how MADD (Mothers Against Drunk Driving) was started:

In 1979, five-and-a-half-month-old Laura Lamb became one of the world's youngest quadriplegics when Laura and her mother, Cindi, were hit head-on by a repeat drunk driving offender traveling at 120 mph. As a result of the crash, Cindi and her friends waged a war against drunk driving in their home state of Maryland. Less than a year later, on the other side of the country in California, 13-year-old Cari Lightner was killed at the hands of a drunk driver. Two days prior, the offender was released on bail for a hit-and-run drunk driving crash. He already had two drunk driving convictions with a third plea-bargained to "reckless accident." At the time of Cari's death, the drunk driving offender was carrying a valid California driver's license.

Enraged, Cari's mother, Candace Lightner, and friends gathered at a steak house in Sacramento. They discussed forming a group named "MADD-Mothers Against Drunk Drivers." Thus, MADD was born with a name that would sweep the nation.

Lightner and Lamb joined forces and by the end of 1981, MADD had 11 chapters in four states...Rounding out 20 years, MADD now has more than 600 chapters in all 50 states and affiliates in Guam, Canada and Puerto Rico.[4]

Anyone who wants to accomplish something great before they punch their final time card in life should listen to Tom Peters, management guru and author of *In Search of Excellence*, who said, "Nothing good or great can be done in the absence of enthusiasm."

What is your passion? Have you buried it in the past, or in the basement? Whatever it is, find it. Whatever it is, do it passionately. "If a man is called to be a streetsweeper," said Martin Luther King, Jr. in one of his famous speeches, "he should sweep streets even as Michelangelo painted, or Beethoven played music, or Shakespeare wrote poetry. He should sweep streets so well that all the hosts of heaven and earth will pause to say, here lived a great streetsweeper who did his job well." Dance. Scribble. Sing. Climb. Fly. Cook. Listen. Play. Whatever you do, do it with enthusiasm, fervor, fire, and zeal.

Do it with passion. And may the Force be with you.

"And in the end, it's not the years in your life that count. It's the life in your years."
–Abraham Lincoln

Live Passionately

1 Act enthusiastic. It is the easiest way to become so.

2 Practice deleting any dull, dead, unhealthy thoughts that creep into your mind so that you can become more receptive to enthusiasm. An effective technique is to write those unwanted thoughts down and burn them. Seriously, there is great cathartic power in that. If you're concerned about burning down the house, write those negative thoughts down, tear them up into little pieces, and flush them down the toilet.

3 Make a tape or CD of some of your favorite energizing songs to listen to while performing some dreaded task. Go to iTunes.com to download a free program for your PC or Mac that will help you organize your music and allow you to create your own playlists and burn them to a CD.

4 Think about when you were young and what you wanted to be when you grew up. What was it? Can you figure out why you might have wanted to be that? (It's usually hidden somewhere behind the colorful spandex and adoring fans.) Now flash forward to the present. Is your current occupation on track with what you imagined for yourself when you were younger? Try to think of some ways that you can move further in that direction.

5 Even if it's just an hour a week, or 15 minutes each day, do whatever you can to try to carve out some extra time for yourself and your favorite hobby. Join a team, take a class, or read a book on your passion, and spend some extra time engaging in it. The newfound enthusiasm just might find its way into the rest of your week as well. But don't make any excuses. Do it. You deserve it. If you can't find 15 minutes a day for yourself, then you have an overblown case of Adultitis and you need to start this book over.

6 It's true that you are who your friends are. Think about the people you know who seem to be naturally enthusiastic and upbeat. Make it a point to spend more time around them, rather than with people who are constantly complaining and pessimistic about everything. There are two sides to every situation. Why not choose to look at the bright side?

7 Do you have a feeling in your gut that you need to make a career change, but aren't quite sure how? Relax. The journey of a thousand miles begins with but one step. And then another. Your passion will give you the energy to get through the challenges. Get yourself a copy of *The*

Path, by Laurie Beth Jones, for help crafting your life's mission statement. It will give you a good blueprint on where to begin.

8 If you're interested in developing your passion or hobby into a career, but are a little uneasy at making the big jump, try to find a way to try it out on a part-time basis. It will give you an opportunity to work out the kinks and discover if you've got a real market. As business picks up, your success and experience will give you the solid footing you need to take the next step.

9 Your passion can be hidden in an issue you care deeply about. What issues are important to you? Find a way to become involved in a charity or organization that focuses on "your" issue.

10 Make sure you allow yourself some time to "get away" once in a while, for a weekend, a day, or even a few uninterrupted hours. Sometimes a little time away is a great way to recharge your batteries and prevent burnout. You'll be able to return to your "regular life" with a new burst of passion.

11 Create a scrapbook or a folder of inspiring pictures, quotations, and articles pertaining to your passion. Use it as a pick-me-up when you are frustrated or discouraged.

Play

"A light heart lives long."

William Shakespeare

As much as I champion the idea of embracing the "inner child," a recent experience helped me to see just how far I have to go. Kim and I were enjoying a beautiful spring day down near Lake Mendota on the University of Wisconsin-Madison campus. It's a great place to go if you enjoy the sport of people-watching. Naturally, we like watching children (although some of the adults walking around there generate an entertainment value like you wouldn't believe).

My eyes locked on a little girl in pigtails, three, maybe four at the most, who was walking along with her parents close behind. Like a magnet pulled to a refrigerator, she immediately gravitated to a rather large puddle, the remnant of an earlier spring rain. Now, she didn't tiptoe through this puddle, she *assaulted* it. If I had to choose two words to describe her interaction with this unsuspecting puddle, gentle and careful would not be among the list of finalists. It was turbulent. Thunderous.

Like watching an inside-out washing machine.

The little girl's explosive encounter with the puddle literally shocked me. Almost everything in my being screamed, "No! What is she *doing!?* Doesn't she know better?"

And it was at that moment when I realized just how grown-up I'd become. While her natural, childlike reaction was to run right through that puddle, mine was undoubtedly to avoid it.

"Egad!" I thought to myself, disgustedly. "What in the world have I become?"

Imagine any city sidewalk on a rainy day, and you will realize that most grown-ups will do anything they can to avoid puddles. Now imagine the same sidewalk filled with children. I can only speculate that there won't be much walking going on, and I doubt very much if any puddles would remain untouched. Moms know: a child has the magical ability to become absolutely drenched from only a Barbie shoe's worth of water.

The incident by the lake presented a mysterious, age-old, chicken-or-the-egg type question: When exactly is the point in our lives when we stop plowing through puddles and start avoiding them? What's the moment when we stop being so carefree and start being so measured and careful? Is it at the age of 10? 16? 23?

Many of you are thinking to yourselves, "That's easy —when we start having to wash our own clothes..."

Granted, muddy laundry is not fun, and it's not recommended to show up for a big quarterly review with wet pants and soggy shoes. But, as we grow up, it's easy to steadily lose

that playful spirit that used to roam as free as a hyperactive butterfly. Look at the way many of us approach vacations, for crying out loud. You know, vacations...those things we take that are supposed to fulfill that instinctive need for play? Even our vacations have become work. We gotta plan for this, be sure to pack that, make certain we can see this and do that, cramming as much "fun" and "joy" as we can into our "relaxing" little vacation. If left unchecked, planning a vacation can make Einsten's Theory of Relativity look like the instructions for chewing bubble gum. And that's not even taking into consideration those of you who wear your beepers on the beach. You know who you are.

I think we can all agree that if there's one thing kids are experts at—it's playing. I look back on my childhood summer days in complete amazement. I don't know how it was possible, but I was *busy*. Extremely busy. My days were packed. With what, you may ask?

Well, I'm not really sure. It's not like I had a Fisher-Price Palm Pilot or anything. But if I had, it would have needed a bigger memory card. My days were absolutely loaded with lots and lots of playing. Any given day could have had me feverishly racing my Ferrari (I mean Spiderman Hot Wheel) up and down the gravel lane, constructing a sprawling urban development made of sticks and sand, or creating Guggenheim-ready works of art on the sidewalk with a few nubs of chalk. When I was five, I had no official job (other than the arduous task of pulling weeds in the driveway for my dad), no bills to pay, and no commitments to run to. But, somehow, I fit so much playing into my day that it was often hard to find time to eat a peanut butter and jelly sandwich.

Come to think of it, I may have been a playaholic. And I bet you were too. (Admission is the first step.)[1]

I wonder how it's possible for a person to become so inept at something at which they were once so good. And not only good at, but an expert, no less. It's like a world-renowned brain surgeon getting to the point where he has trouble locating the skull. Or a .300 hitter running to third base on a ground ball up the middle. It's sad, really sad.

"You have to grow up sometime," you might be saying. "Life isn't all fun and games." That may be true, but neither is play. A publication by the Alliance for Childhood, a partnership of educators, health care professionals, and researchers, points out that "decades of research demonstrate that play—active and full of imagination—is more than just fun and games. It boasts a healthy development across a broad spectrum of critical areas: intellectual, social, emotional, and physical."[2] In fact, experts in child development say that plenty of time for childhood play is one of the key factors leading to happiness in adulthood.[3]

There's no doubt play is important for kids, but its usefulness does not wear out as our gray hairs grow in. We all know that life doesn't get any easier. Life is filled with ups and downs, twists and turns. Think about the story of a little boy who went to the grocery store and asked the clerk for a box of detergent. The clerk asked why he needed the detergent.

> The usefulness of play does not wear out as our gray hairs grow in.

"I want to wash my dog," replied the lad.

"Well, son, this detergent is

pretty strong for washing a little dog."

The little boy replied, "That's what I want. He's mighty dirty."

He took the box of detergent home, and about a week later he returned. The store clerk, recognizing him, asked him about his dog. "Oh, he's dead," said the boy.

"I'm sorry," replied the clerk. "I guess the detergent was too strong."

"I don't think the detergent hurt him," said the boy. "I think it was the rinse cycle that got him."[4]

Life has a way of putting us through the wash, so to speak. Sooner or later, it's the rinse cycle that gets us. I can't help but wonder how many fewer heart attacks we'd see in this country if we took more time to play as adults. God knows we could use it. In fact, statistics show that stress has been linked to all of the leading causes of death, including heart disease, cancer, lung ailments, accidents, cirrhosis, and suicide. It has been calculated that 75-90% of all visits to primary care physicians are for stress-related complaints or disorders.[5] I wonder if that has anything to do with the fact that we spend less time playing. I don't believe for one second that play is only for kids. Humorist Josh Billings said it perfectly, "There ain't much fun in medicine, but there's a heck of a lot of medicine in fun."

In *The Journal of Personality and Social Psychology*, Alice Isen wrote about a study in which two groups of college students watched a video before being assigned to solve several creative problems. The first group of students watched a tape filled with bloopers and highlights of old comedy shows. The second group watched a math video called *Area Under A Curve*

(I can only imagine the seat-gripping suspense emanating from that film). As it turned out, the students in the first group, who were in a good mood from all the laughing, ended up being 300 to 500 percent more likely to come up with successful solutions to the problems they were given.

The need to play is built right into us. It's a custom-made stress release valve. We've gotten a little out of practice, however. Did you know that preschoolers laugh up to 450 times a day? That's a lot of knock-knock jokes. The average adult laughs just 15 times a day. Aside from the sticky hands and endless bathroom stops, with whom would you rather make a cross-country trip? I'd say our biggest problem is that we don't understand, or take for granted, how much value play holds, and often relegate it to a level light-years lower than that of work. We often look at play as "unproductive," and thus it has a hard time making it onto our cluttered to-do lists. We can be made to feel guilty if we bypass some work to toss around the Frisbee®, enjoy a captivating novel, partake in a leisurely walk on a fall day, or book a cruise to the Bahamas.

As great as play is for children, it is equally important for us grown-ups. That's because play teaches us how to manage and transform our "negative" emotions and experiences, it supercharges learning, and is a foundational factor in good mental and physical health. It can make work pleasurable instead of drudgery. And beyond all the excellent reasons for playing, there is simply the sheer fun of it. A lot of good can be said for getting our fair measure of play.[6]

Moms are especially guilty when it comes to gipping themselves out of some much-needed play time. Admirably, they typically put everyone else's needs above their own. But if you've ever been on a plane—and actually paid attention to the pre-flight safety procedures—you'd know that the flight attendants have very specific instructions when it comes to the oxygen masks. If you're traveling with children, the attendants always tell you to put the mask on yourself first. That way you'll be better able to care for your children. I'm not saying that moms should do a 180 and always put themselves first—where would we be without you?—but doesn't it make sense that they'd be able to take better care of their kids if they took time out for a bubble bath once in a while?

We need to play. We need to live life to the fullest. And a life lived without an abundance of laughter and playfulness is one that has been seriously shortchanged. What's the saying?... "All work and no play makes Jack a dull and boring heart attack candidate?" (Or something to that effect.) Play decreases stress levels and provides us with the energy we need to tackle the never-ending to-do list. It's always easier to accomplish things when you're not "white-knuckling" it.

Michael LeBoeuf, Ph.D., says, "Most stress is caused by people who overestimate the importance of their problems." Again we see a classic symptom of Adultitis. For the most part, we just seem to be so serious about everything. When I get uptight or anxious about something, I try to ask myself the question, "Will it matter five years from now?" In most cases, there's a pretty easy answer. Most of the things I worry about won't matter five breakfasts from now. It's a fact: most things are not as serious as we make them out to be. And that includes ourselves.

Part of being a good "play-er" consists of not taking yourself too seriously. I think back to high school and all the effort I put into worrying about what others thought of me. There were about 300 kids in my graduating class, and I have only occasional contact with a small handful today. We spend an awful lot of time worrying about what other people think of us. Not kids. Want proof? I submit as evidence the wardrobe selection of a child who is finally free to make his own clothing choices for the day. Far from matching, a child's self-chosen outfit borders on ridiculous. It may consist of a tank top, Hawaiian shorts, a headband, cowboy boots, a crown, and a pair of aviator sunglasses... and that's just before noon. I doubt that any child would object to wearing a Spiderman costume to church.

Want an exercise in not taking yourself too seriously? Tomorrow morning, before you take your shower, make your way into the bathroom and strip naked. That's a good time because it's a recommended step before taking a shower anyway. Take a good look at yourself in the mirror, and then start singing. Sing "On Top of Spaghetti." I guarantee you won't have any trouble not taking yourself seriously. And you'll probably start your day with a good chuckle.

Naked bodies and mirrors work wonders, but interestingly, I've noticed that it is children—especially babies—who have a unique ability to draw grown-ups out of the mindset of worrying what others think. Perfectly sane adults make some of the most embarrassing and downright silly faces as they coo over a baby. Like carefree drunks, they lose their ability to speak coherently, and contort their faces in such a way as to make Jim Carrey jealous. The strange and cool thing is that this behavior is perfectly acceptable, anytime, anyplace. But it's not just babies who have this power over adults.

I remember my dad playing with my niece when she was about four. She'd lead him around the house and yard, going from one activity to another. At any given point, I could look up and see him lying flat on his back getting imaginary shots, wearing some sort of princess tiara, or helping Barbie and Ken drive their new pink Corvette to the grocery store. Priceless moments that I wish I had photographed, if for no other reason than to use them in a sinister blackmail scheme. But beyond the silliness, when looking closer, it's as if the child was teaching the grown-up how to play. In most cases, the grown-up is surprised by just how much fun it is.

Okay, by now you should understand the important benefits of regular and spontaneous play. But I imagine the idea of scribbling on the front sidewalk or playing with plastic dolls may leave you a bit uneasy. If that's the case, play is not what you think it is.

Most of all, play is a state of being. Everybody has his or her own favorite ways to play. The Institute for Play goes so far as to list a variety of play personalities, such as The Explorer, The Artist, The Collector, The Craftsman, and more. I would recommend checking out http://www.instituteforplay.com for more information and to discover your play personality.

There are different types of play that involve a wide range of activities. Do you enjoy reading romance novels? Downhill skiing? Cheering your favorite sports team to victory? Getting together for drinks with friends? Writing short stories? Collecting antiques? Building furniture? Spending time in your vegetable garden? All of these activities are considered playful (if you enjoy doing them, that is), and I promise you that you'll be less stressed-out and happier if you schedule more time for them. Yes, some of us have gotten so out of shape when it comes to playing, it is absolutely necessary to schedule time for it. We're so used to scheduling everything else into our busy lives that anything left off the list is left in the dust.

Back when we were dating, Kim and I had a little game that helps demonstrate how the idea of play can be simply built into any relationship. We had a small, plastic Pokey (of Gumby® fame) that we took turns hiding from each other. I would hide it under her pillow, in her shoe, or in

Some of us have gotten so out of shape when it comes to playing, it is absolutely necessary to schedule time for it.

her coat pocket. When she'd find it, she'd invariably smile, and then hide it in a place I'd least expect, like in my box of Frosted Flakes®.

As you tap back into your God-given ability to play (remember, that thing you were once an expert in?), you'll no doubt get better at finding opportunities to engage in spontaneous play, which is the best kind. My parents do a great job in this area. They like going on rides together, mostly to nowhere in particular. They like the good scenery and the stimulating conversation, which I am sure has been a major contributor to the strength of their marriage. It is not uncommon for them to take a spur-of-the-moment weekend getaway. One time, they went to breakfast with the intention of going to a particular small town. Conversation over the eggs and toast, and some advice from the waitress, inspired them to travel several hundred miles in the opposite direction instead. Nothing about it was planned, except for the decision to get away from the daily grind for a while.

Sometimes you just need to get away to recharge your energy levels and boost your productivity. Louis Dembitz Brandeis was a United States Supreme Court Justice who understood this concept perfectly. He was once criticized for taking a short vacation just before the start of an important trial. "I need the rest," explained Brandeis. "I find that I can do a year's work in eleven months, but I can't do it in twelve."[7] Similarly, preacher Vance Havner said, "Unless we come apart and rest a while, we may just plain come apart."

To me, the stuff in this chapter just makes sense. And it has a great deal of scientific research to back it up. But I am constantly amazed at the people who just don't get it. The dad who works countless hours at the office, missing his child's first steps. The mom who puts so much effort into taking care of the kids, but won't make some time for herself to curl up with a good book or soak in a tub full of bubbles. The grad student who is so caught up in doing research for his doctorate that he doesn't try catching snowflakes on his tongue on his way to the library.

Play is a big part of what I do. One of the main concepts behind my comic strip, *Kim & Jason,* is (not surprisingly) the idea of Escaping Adulthood. It is my hope that by reading the strip, people will be encouraged to think more like children, and tackle the stresses of the day with a childlike spirit. Our web site and product line all revolve around this central theme. But sometimes, people just don't get it.

One day, one of our "Sales Servants"[8] visited a little gift shop to see if the owner would be interested in carrying our product line. The store had a whimsical quality to it, indicating that it might be a good fit. The Sales Servant pulled out one of our catalogs, which happened to have "Escape Adulthood" displayed on the cover. After only a few moments of hearing about the mission behind *Kim & Jason,* the owner coldly exclaimed, "I don't believe in that. I happen to think that we're adults now, and that's a good thing, and we should just concentrate on that."

Yikes.

I submit this as an example of someone who probably could stand to give herself some time to play. Needless to say, we didn't make the sale.

 Play

1 Break free from the boring cubicle—bring some of your favorite toys to work and arrange them in your workspace.

2 Make sure to schedule at least a few hours each week for play. Spend it doing something fun, something that interests you. If you're out of practice, you'll need to write it down in your planner or enter it into your PDA, or else it probably won't happen.

3 Next time you go out to eat, order dessert first.

4 Buy a bag of jumbo marshmallows the next time you're at the store. Then, with some friends or family members, begin a rousing installment of "Chubby Bunny." Contestants take turns stuffing their mouths with marshmallows, then they try to say, "chubby bunny." The winner is the one who can still spout the phrase without spewing marshmallows everywhere. It's great fun and a wonderful tension reliever.

---

5 Speaking of tension relievers, laughter is still the best medicine. Go to a live comedy show, or rent one of

your favorite movies (check out the Three Stooges or the Little Rascals for some really good laughs). Many comedians also have their stand-up routines available on CD and cassette. It's great stuff to listen to on the way to work. Read the funny pages. If *Kim & Jason* isn't in your local paper, first call the editor and complain. Then go to KimandJason.com to sign up to receive the comic strip via e-mail absolutely free.

6 Test drive a car you can't afford.

7 When was the last time you jumped into a pile of leaves? The healing power is remarkable. If you have kids, join them in the fun. If you don't have kids, wait 'til the neighbors are away (if you're uncomfortable having them see you). It will be worth it.

8 On your next vacation, try to leave the beeper, cell phone and PDA at home. If just the thought of it scares you senseless, this is especially crucial for you. Give it a try and allow yourself to focus on everything the time away has to offer. The other stuff will be there when you get back, and you'll be amazed at how much more easily you'll be able to handle it.

9 Watch the movie *Patch Adams*, starring Robin Williams, to see both the positive effects of playing and the disastrous effects of *not* playing.

10 Next time you're with a friend or two, turn the TV to an old sitcom and turn down the sound. Make up your own dialogue for the show.

11 Come up with your own version of the "Hide Pokey" game with a friend or loved one. It's a neat way to build a lot of fun and playfulness into your relationship without a ton of effort.

Be Honest

"The true measure of life is not length, but honesty."

John Lyly

The checkout line resembles rush hour traffic on a New York City bridge. Long, snarled, and sedentary. You wonder how in the world it's physically possible to have stood in a line for twenty minutes and actually be FARTHER from the checkout. You scan the tabloids to pass the time, and after one too many stories of alien abductions and people born with hooves, you think to yourself, "At least I'm not having *that* bad of a day."

And you're right. That is until your daughter, who is sitting in the shopping cart, stares and points at a larger gentlemen with hairy arms and loudly proclaims, "Hey, that guy looks like a big gorilla."

Suddenly, if faced with the decision, you'd choose hooves.

Every parent probably has a similar story to share, primarily because of the undeniable truth: left to their own devices, children are unequivocally honest. We all started out in life expressing our true feelings freely and spontaneously.

My mother-in-law re-learned that little tidbit recently. She was having a conversation with her grandson, talking about things that interest little boys. Suddenly he stopped, and thoughtfully said, "Grandma, did you know you have grey hair?"

"Yes, Tristan, I am aware of that," responded Grandma.

"No. *Really* grey. You should look in the mirror. And you have a yellow tooth, too."

Heartfelt advice from a kindergartner.

I once knew a young Sunday school teacher who struggled

with acne. One day she told me how one of the little girls casually diagnosed the teacher with chicken pox. "No, I don't have chicken pox," assured the teacher. But the girl insisted. "Yes you do. They're all over your face! There's a chicken pock here, and here, and here…"

My wife has what I would describe as an alarming fingernail biting problem. One day at school, as she was helping a student with a lesson, the little boy pointed at her fingers, looked up at her, and said, "Eeww."

Truth be told, kids are naturally honest. To a fault, some would say (especially grandmas and grown men who resemble gorillas).

When my wife was in first grade at a private school, she was given a distinct honor. As Kim got off the bus, a priest singled her out. He asked her to speak during the homily of a Catholic Schools Week Mass celebrated by three area schools. The sermon was on "change" and Kim was the first of several children who were presented with the question, "Of anything in the world, what would you most like to change?"

Kim was excited for the opportunity. Calmly and confidently, Kim stepped up to the microphone and said, "I'd like to change my room around." This was a natural response, considering that she would always beg her mother for permission to switch the furniture around in her bedroom.

The next girl said she'd make it so nobody ever got sick. It didn't take long for Kim to realize that her answer was a bit off, but you've got to admire her honesty. At least one reporter did, because her quote ended up in the paper.

Kids start out pretty honest, but I think they usually learn the fine art of lying from us grown-ups. It's not that we maliciously intend to warp their little minds, but we often can't seem to refrain from telling those little white lies. Like when we tell them that something "won't hurt a bit" when it really feels like some form of medieval torture. Or that the local toy store no longer sells Barbies® of any kind. Or we promise that we'll play that riveting game of Candyland® later, secretly knowing that in this case, later means...never.[1]

Even though children are naturally honest—sometimes scathingly so—it is crucial that we make a concerted effort to model for them the importance of honesty. Our efforts with them when they are very young can last a lifetime. For instance, Allan C. Emery, a very successful businessman, commented on the impact his father made on him in his book *A Turtle On A Fencepost*:

> "Once [my dad] lost a pair of fine German binoculars. He collected the insurance only to find the binoculars a year later. Immediately, he sent a check to the company and received a letter back stating that this seldom occurred and that they were encouraged. It was a small thing, but children never forget examples lived before them."[2]

My own father has been a model of honesty in my life. After enjoying a meal at a restaurant and upon the arrival of the check, it is not uncommon for my dad to find an error in which he has been undercharged. Many people would take the attitude of "their error, their loss," but not my dad. He has the situation corrected, even if it only amounts to a few cents.

He manages a lumberyard, and he often picks out materials from inventory to bring home for various home improvement projects. Since he has the keys to the office, he is able to pick up a few pints of stain or a bundle of plywood at his convenience. But even if he makes a late-night run for last minute supplies, he never ever leaves the office without first filling out a ticket documenting the transaction. That's the kind of person my dad is, and it has shaped my own moral code.

As I sit and marvel at his integrity, I am struck by the fact that he wasn't always such an angel, and that he, too, must have gotten some guidance on the importance of honesty as he grew up. I can recall one story he has told a million times concerning a grade-school report card.

As a wee lad, my dad went to a Catholic school that was just a few blocks from his house. The strict standards of the nuns who ran the school were only matched by those of my grandmother. Not exactly the most "gifted" student, my dad had indulged in more than his fair share of, shall we say, screwing around. When the quarter was up and report cards were handed out, he accordingly received his fair share of poor marks, including a few failing grades. Of course, the report cards had to be turned back in with the signature of both parents, indicating that they had indeed seen the progress (or lack thereof) of their little angels.

My dad was petrified. He knew that the low scores would not bring glad tidings. Being a quick thinker, he found two gold foil stickers—two shiny stars. He carefully put one over each of the two failing marks, firmly enough so they wouldn't fall off, yet carefully enough to be removed at a later (more convenient) time. When she saw the report card, his mother of course inquired about the stars. My dad explained in so many words that they were a new symbol that showed above-exemplary progress. She proudly signed her name to the card; on the way to school the next day, he carefully peeled the stars away and chucked them to the wind. When his teacher asked him for his parents' reaction when he turned in the report card, he mumbled something about needing to work harder. The report card in question was found in a box when we cleaned out my grandma's house after she passed away. It still had two gold stars clinging on for dear life, as the cover-up had to be repeated each quarter. It is still not known how many packages of gold foil stars Dad went through that school year.

I am thankful that my dad encountered some guidance as he grew up that helped shape his character, and ultimately mine as well. It is critical that we, as parents, teachers and citizens, do our part to instruct children in the areas of right and wrong, because even though they have a natural propensity for honesty, they, like the pint-size version of my father, have been given mixed messages.

A 1998 Reuters news story tells how a New York City cab driver and Mayor Rudolph Giuliani helped give schoolchildren a lesson in honesty:

NEW YORK (Reuters) - A group of schoolchildren gave Mayor Rudolph Giuliani the wrong answer about honesty Monday as he thanked a Pakistani taxi driver for returning more than $10,000 in lost cash to a Belgian tourist.

Syed Shah, 33, found $10,042, a Belgian passport and

a leather bag in his cab late Friday night and reported it to the police. The money was returned to an elderly woman tourist, who was not identified by authorities.

"Now, if you found that money what would you do?" Giuliani asked the children, guests for the morning at City Hall. "Keeeep iiiiitt!" they replied in singsong unison. With the audience laughing, the mayor told the elementary schoolchildren, "No, no, the reason we have Mr. Shah here is to teach you a different answer. If you found that money and it wasn't yours, you should return it. Only bad people keep things that don't belong to them," Giuliani said.

Shah, who immigrated to New York six years ago, said his Muslim upbringing taught him to be honest. "I am a religious person and my religion teaches me that I am supposed to be nice to other people," Shah said. "If I had kept the money I would feel guilty my whole life."[3]

Even people who grow up to be President of the United States need to be schooled in the area of honesty from time to time. In his book about George W. Bush, Stephen Mansfield tells of a time in the future President's youth when a family friend took him to a museum. The young boy stood with eyes like saucers as he looked at the large dinosaur skeleton in the museum's collection. He was excited to go home and tell his mother. Upon recounting the details of his adventure, he proudly pulled out a brown paper bag that contained bones he had taken from the dinosaur's tail. George's parents made sure the bones were quickly returned.[4]

A friend of my family had a neat way of teaching the importance of honesty to her kids. She told them, "I trust you. I will always believe that what you say is true. But if I ever catch you in a lie, it will take a long time to earn back that trust. If you lie to me once, then how will I ever know when you *are* telling the truth?"

Sadly, a recent *USA Today* poll found that only 56 percent of Americans teach honesty to their children. Our current state of world affairs is fraught with the consequences of lies, deceptions, and half-truths. I wonder what it would look like if we tried to bring a bit more honesty into our lives. We could all be challenged by giving ourselves a little self-honesty test: Do I always do the right thing, even if no one else is watching? Can I always be counted on to follow through and do what I said I'd do? Do I ever take things I don't deserve, like awards, money, praise, or credit for an idea? Do I always mean what I say and say what I mean? Answering these questions presents a tall order for anyone to respond to, but that doesn't make honesty any less worthy an aim.

> Only 56 percent of Americans teach honesty to their children.

Honesty is certainly in short demand these days, in politics, in the media, and in business. This lack of rectitude has left us all jaded and cynical, often leading us to doubt nearly everything we hear. With high-profile court cases, political cover-ups, corporate scandals, and extra-marital affairs becoming so commonplace, we're sometimes left scratching

our heads wondering if anyone tells the truth anymore. We're bombarded with spam, promising bigger this and smaller that. Diet gurus promise instant weight loss, and drug companies promise instant relief (at an outrageous price). Computer viruses come to us disguised as friendly messages from our closest friends. Politicians spin facts in order to get a rise in the polls and use the polls to compensate for their own lack of honest opinion. Will it ever end?

Dishonesty certainly has its consequences. St. Augustine warned, "When regard for truth has been broken down or even slightly weakened, all things will remain doubtful." Dishonesty often leads to ruined political careers, disgraced reputations, and vacations to bright and sunny federal penitentiaries. And remember, things didn't turn out very well for the boy who cried wolf.

Frankly, dishonesty is easy. Opportunities to be dishonest seem to be plentiful. Consider the schoolteacher who asked a struggling student during an exam, "Ken, how close are you to the right answer?"

"About two seats," he replied.

Yes, dishonesty is easy; it can even be profitable. As someone once said, "They say honesty pays, but it doesn't seem to pay enough to suit most people." But although a lie is easy, a guilty conscience sure can make it hard to sleep soundly at night. And even though some businesses have profited handsomely from dishonest business practices, others have discovered how rewarding it can be to admit weaknesses in their own advertising in order to highlight their strengths. It's a fresh approach that builds trust and goodwill with consumers who are starved for sincerity and integrity.

Consider a study conducted on salespeople:

"In 1982, the Forum Corporation of Boston, Massachusetts, studied 341 salespeople from eleven different companies in five different industries. The purpose of their study was to determine what accounted for the difference between the top producers and the average producers. Guess what, when the study was finished, it was not skill, knowledge, or charisma that separated the best from the average. Forum Corporation found the difference was attributable to honesty. When customers can trust salespeople, they will buy from them."[5]

Pro wrestler turned political virtuoso Jesse Ventura surprised just about everyone when he was elected as Minnesota's governor. As a youthful wrestling fan, I remember watching "The Body" in the ring, and later at ringside as an announcer. He was always known for "telling it like it is." I think that was the quality he successfully carried over to politics, and what resonated with people who voted for him. Just as with a five-year-old, where you're never quite sure what will be said but are quite sure that it probably won't be very tactful, you at least know where the guy stands.

Dr. Phil McGraw has built a veritable empire on being honest. People who have read his books or seen the fiery Texan on TV have no doubts about his honesty. He's another person known for telling it like it is. Is he entertaining? You bet. It's as entertaining as hearing someone *else's* daughter call someone in a supermarket checkout line a gorilla. But Dr. Phil has helped a lot of people in the process of being blunt.

> Honesty and integrity are positive traits that will not only follow you everywhere you go, they will also precede you.

Honesty and integrity are positive traits that will not only follow you everywhere you go, they will also precede you.

Truly, honesty is the cornerstone of character. The best way to develop such a remarkable character is to make a commitment to telling the truth.

A reporter once asked a politician, "Sir, you probably see over a hundred people every day. You answer each one of them with a 'Yes' or 'No' or 'Maybe.' I've never seen you write any notes, but I've also never heard you forgetting what you promised them. What is your secret?"

The politician looked squarely in the eye of the reporter and answered, "If you tell the truth the first time, you don't have to remember."[6]

Honest politicians are hard to come by – the legend of George Washington refusing to tell a lie after cutting down the cherry tree is just that, a legend. But Abraham Lincoln was a man who certainly lived up to his nickname, "Honest Abe." Author Adam Kahn outlines a few anecdotes in his book, *Self-Help Stuff That Works*:

Abraham Lincoln was honest. During his years as a lawyer, there were hundreds of documented examples of his honesty and decency. For example, Lincoln didn't like to charge people much who were as poor as he was. Once a man sent him twenty-five dollars, but Lincoln sent him back ten of it, saying he was being too generous.

He was known at times to convince his clients to settle their issues out of court, saving them a lot of money, and earning himself nothing.

An old woman in dire poverty, the widow of a Revolutionary soldier, was charged $200 for getting her $400 pension.

Lincoln sued the pension agent and won the case for the old woman. He didn't charge her for his services and, in fact, paid her hotel bill and gave her money to buy a ticket home!

He and his associate once prevented a con man from gaining possession of a tract of land owned by a mentally ill girl. The case took fifteen minutes. Lincoln's associate came to divide up their fee, but Lincoln reprimanded him. His associate argued that the girl's brother had agreed on the fee ahead of time, and he was completely satisfied.

"That may be," said Lincoln, "but I am not satisfied. That money comes out of the pocket of a poor, demented girl; I would rather starve than swindle her in this manner. You return half the money at least, or I'll not take a cent of it as my share."

Lincoln didn't talk much about religion, even with his best friends, and he didn't belong to any church. But he once confided to a friend that his religious code was the same as an old man he knew in Indiana, who said, "When I do good, I feel good, and when I do bad, I feel bad, and that's my religion."[7]

Someone once said that real success is to be admired by children and adults alike. People of high integrity and deep honesty enjoy that kind of admiration. But it is important that we are not only truthful with others, we really need to be honest with ourselves. The truth is an interesting thing. As much as we may not want to believe it, truth is absolute and unchanging. We can spin and rationalize and theorize all day long, but truth is truth. Winston Churchill said, "The truth is inconvertible, malice may attack it, ignorance may deride it, but in the end, there it is."

Perhaps we can use Churchill as a humorous example of how to be unabashedly honest. Once when he was visiting the White House, President Roosevelt made his way to Churchill's bedroom and opened the door unexpectedly. Churchill was standing in the middle of the room, stark naked and completely unembarrassed. "You see, Mr. President," he said, "We British have nothing to hide."[8]

Alcoholics can only begin recovery when they admit they have a problem. People can only lose weight when they admit that they eat too much and don't exercise enough. We can think with all of our might that we aced a test, but all the excuses and rationalization in the world will never turn an F to an A. In order to see real change in our lives, it is imperative that we be honest with ourselves. The truth can be tough to swallow, but ignoring it doesn't make it any less true. Dr. Phil has it right. "Get real" is his way of saying, "Let's be honest with ourselves, people!"

> In order to see real change in our lives, it is imperative that we be honest with ourselves.

If we try to set an example of honesty even in the simplest matters, we will find that honesty is a powerful catalyst for good in this world. It helps to connect us all. One of the reasons Charles Schulz had such a hit on his hands with *Peanuts* is because of Charlie Brown, his lovable loser. He always said, correctly, that humor is found in tragedy, not victory. That's why it took so many years for Charlie Brown to finally win a baseball game. People could relate and respond to Charlie's mishaps and failures because they were candid and real.

Music is a big part of our lives. I have certain songs that I consider the "soundtrack of my life." The songs that I hold most dear to my heart are often the most honest, the ones that cut beyond candy-coated superficiality and speak to some deeper truth. Those are the ones that remind me of particular experiences I've had and how I felt about them at the time. Maybe you could create a similar list.

One of the reasons Spiderman is so popular with people is because the hero is not some perfect specimen from another planet, but rather a genuine portrayal of a struggling, self-conscious teen trying to make his way in the world. We can relate to Peter Parker, even though we can't effortlessly scale skyscrapers.

This world needs us to be honest with each other, honest with ourselves, and to demand honesty from those around us. Are we required to point out that our boss seems to have put on a few pounds, or that our wife is having a really bad hair day? I certainly wouldn't recommend that. But I do recommend looking deep within ourselves in an honest fashion, and striving to model a consistent honesty that will leave us with admirable integrity.

May I suggest that it would be far worse to be a man with shallow integrity and able hands than one with limitless integrity and hooves.

P.S. My sister-in-law Kristy placed a very high emphasis on the value of honesty as she grew up. When she was little, she was uncommonly sensitive towards others and felt it was very important to have it known that she meant what she said. Whenever she wrote a complimentary message in a birthday card or letter, she always followed up with "P.S. Everything is true."

 Be Honest

 The next time you find that you have inadvertently shorted someone, be sure to point out the error and settle up (no matter how big or small).

 Always keep a perspective on the consequences of a little white lie (remember Enron). It can often be very hard (or impossible) to recover from the destruction that a lie can bring.

 My wife gives me a hard time with this one, but it is difficult for me to say something nice about something if I really don't believe it. If my friend dyes her hair blue, I don't want to lie and say it looks great. Instead, I'll say something like, "It's quite a dramatic difference," or "I've always admired your individualistic personality." Perhaps it's semantics, but maybe it will work for you, too.

 Make sure to always be a model of honesty to your children. Even if you don't have children of your own, the children around you are looking to you for an example on how to behave. Try to be a good example; it can have long-term effects.

5 Spend some time around kids to get an appreciation for their honesty. And if they're not your kids, it can be quite entertaining.

6 You can reward honesty by granting special privileges to a child, acknowledging an employee, or voting for a candidate who has acted forthrightly.

7 Model Abe Lincoln's behavior, and always act humbly and honestly, particularly with someone in a position lower than yours, especially when other people aren't watching, and even if "conventional" wisdom is on your side.

8 Keep company with people who are honest. Your reputation can be ruined if you are linked to a person or group caught lying or cheating, even if you weren't at fault.

9 If you're caught in a lie—we've all been there—'fess up as soon as possible. People are more willing to forgive someone who offers a contrite confession than someone who goes to great lengths to cover it up.

10 If you are in business, make sure you are always truthful with your customers and shareholders. In this competitive age, a strong brand and a trusted reputation are priceless.

Finally, be honest about yourself. Don't get caught in the trap of blaming others for unpleasant circumstances in which you might find yourself. Certainly, extenuating, uncontrollable circumstances affect our lives, but you'll be able to turn things around much more quickly by acknowledging your own shortcomings and moving to correct them.

Have Faith

"Believe in something greater than yourself."

Barbara Bush

I can't help but wonder: what do the monsters under the bed do during the day? Where do they go? Do they spend the time plotting evil new ways to cook and season little boys? Do they update the scoreboard that tallies the screams of the children of the world? Or do they perhaps browse the scareology section of the local used bookstore for the latest bargains and bestsellers?

Their daytime agenda may be a mystery, but their modus operandi is not. Under the bright rays of daylight, that space under your bed reveals nothing but emptiness, save a few missing game pieces and a discarded sock. But as soon as the sun goes down and the bedroom light goes out, the shadows slowly crawl up the wall and you hear what seems to be the sound of breathing come from at least one or two hideous, slovenly beasts waiting for an opening. An opportunity. If your foot should happen to accidentally drift over the side of the bed, you certainly won't live to regret it.

Thank God for the night-light—that dependable guardian of safety—faithfully providing just enough illumination to keep the monsters at bay. Because we all know they just HATE the light.

Being an anxious young lad, I had even more on my mind than those monsters. Apparently one fear wasn't enough—I had to have a full stable of them. It was part of what became a ritual of sorts. My dad would come in after I had nestled into bed, with the customary glass of cold water. After taking a swig, I confided—every night as if it were the first time—that I was afraid of the Thunder and the Lightning and the Fire Trucks.

The original Axis of Evil.

And, every night – as if it were the first time – my father would calmly say, "That's okay, Jason, they're all in bed now." And for some reason, somehow, that was enough for me. I was as sure as the snow is white that the Thunder and the Lightning and the Fire Trucks were indeed in bed (of course never stopping to consider what type of beds those might be. Perhaps triple-decker bunk beds?). With that confident assurance—and the steady glow of the night light—I was able to drift off into dreamland.[1]

Isn't that how it goes with kids, though? The word of Mom and Dad is golden, more reliable than a hot summer in San Antonio. If your dad informs you that babies come from storks, then who can argue? When you skin your knee on the unforgiving sidewalk, and Mom kisses your boo-boo, is it not instantly healed? Kids seem to have an inherent ability to have faith in something bigger than themselves. They trust that their parents know everything and are pretty much on the same level as any of your better-known superheroes.

As we grow up, we begin to see that, in reality, our parents are flawed, confused, and at least a little psychotic (just like us). But that doesn't mean that there isn't still something much bigger than us, looking out for us, and loving us without condition. That seems to get lost in the details of living, as we take the weight of the world on our own shoulders. We worry about our strained marriage, our job security (or lack thereof) and paying the mortgage. We lie awake at night wondering if we're good-enough parents. We fret about big life changes, which become increasingly indistinguishable from the host of little ones.

Why do we do that? Why do we have trouble believing that there is a God who created us, who is absolutely in love with us, who REALLY cares about all the little insignificant details of our day? For some of us, God is an afterthought, something way out there somewhere, much too busy to be concerned about our paltry problems. For others, God isn't thought of at all. There are a lot of people who don't know much about God. I don't think that's God's fault. I agree with Martin R. DeHaan II, president of Radio Bible Class Ministries, who said, "The God who made the world has no trouble being seen and heard by those who honestly want to know him."

I certainly don't want to turn this chapter into a philosophical argument on the existence of God. If you've made it this far, you know where I stand. I find it fascinating that children don't seem to have any problem knowing God. In fact, they seem to have a natural awareness built right in. I am reminded of a story of a girl who liked to sneak into her little sister's nursery to ask her if she remembered what heaven was like.

There is another story I once heard in which a mother had just put her six-year-old daughter to sleep, and a little while later, noticed the child was quite restless. She seemed to be sad and upset, so the mom entered the room to see what was the matter. "Mommy, I'm starting to forget," said the little girl.

"What are you starting to forget?"

The girl replied, "I'm starting to forget what it was like when I was with God, before I came here."[2]

My wife Kim has overheard many highly philosophical conversations in her kindergarten class over the years. She once heard some children discussing biblical stories, with one little girl stating that the Devil killed Jesus, but then Jesus killed the Devil. Another expressive boy enjoyed singing songs about Noah, his ark, God, and of course, Beezus. The theology is a bit off, but the awareness is there.

> "The God who made the world has no trouble being seen and heard by those who honestly want to know him."
>
> -Martin R. DeHaan II

In our monster-under-the-bed scenario, it's plain to see when the lights are on and bedtime is hours away, that there are no gremlins under the bed. I look at the light as a symbol of faith. When our bedroom is flooded with sunlight, there are no monsters to be found. That's how it is in life. With a strong faith to light the way, our fears and worries melt away. But as night falls, or our faith wavers, we are much more easily frightened by the distorted shadows of our imaginations.

Yes, our imaginations.

I wholeheartedly subscribe to the idea I once heard that fear is no more than **F**alse **E**vidence **A**ppearing **R**eal. If we

----

were honest with ourselves (there's that honesty thing again), we would realize that most of the things we spend time worrying about have no basis in reality, and never even end up coming true.

We can be confident in knowing that even the tiniest night light sheds enough radiance to keep the monsters at bay. Think of a tiny match. It seems small and insignificant. But with one strike, it can quickly bring light to an entire room and even become a raging fire. As such, we only need a tiny spark of faith to provide us with the peace that God is there, and He's got our back.

When you're a kid, whenever you're out in public, you're usually holding your parent's hand. Whether you're crossing the street or at the mall, Dad's got your hand in his, embracing it tightly. It's hard to feel safer. And it provides another nice fringe benefit—you're free to check out the scenery. Without having to watch for cars, or keep an eye out for where you're going, you get to count the cracks in the sidewalk, stare at the funny-looking guy with the bushy mustache, and look for loose change. Best of all, you always end up in the right place.

I usually start each weekday with a brisk walk. It helps me to get my head on straight before I tackle the day. This may sound silly, but sometimes I imagine God is there, walking with me and holding my hand, just like my parents used to do. I get a great feeling of peace as any anxiety seems to be lifted away. The security of His presence gives me the freedom to look around as I walk, noticing the little things that I would normally miss. On days like this, the scenery is always spectacular and it always feels good to be alive.[3]

We may be all "grown-up" now (whatever that means), but I can't help thinking that God still wants us to be holding someone's hand—His. How much better would life be if we didn't have to worry so much about where we were going and had more freedom to enjoy the scenery? It's not an easy thing to do, because we want to control things. We wonder, who knows where we should be headed better than us? What if He leads us down the wrong road?

He won't. He's got a pretty good handle on things. And He has a better sense of direction than your mom (Dad's in third place, by the way; we all know most dads traditionally don't fare well in this category). We can be very confident that if we take hold of His hand, He'll get us where we need to go.

> How much better would life be if we didn't have to worry so much about where we were going and had more freedom to enjoy the scenery?

I have experienced God's navigational abilities firsthand in my life. I am blown away by the surprises and opportunities God has given to me; surprises and opportunities I would never have found on my own. I have questioned Him, yes, but in the long run, the place I end up turns out to be an even better place than I could have imagined. I have tried my best to put my faith in Him, and He has not failed me.

Starting a business is a scary proposition. In the early days, Kim and I often struggled with financial worries. Would her teaching salary be enough to support us? Would the business succeed, or would we end up in a big pile of debt? Would our financial risks pay off in the long run? Ultimately, we budgeted wisely and trusted God to take care of the rest. We committed to being generous with the little we had, and God repaid us time and time again. Every time a big financial cri-

sis loomed, like when our van had to get a new "everything" put in, an unexpected check would come in the mail, keeping us afloat. Kim has often said that she really wants to try to outgive God, but so far, we've been pretty ineffective.

The mere act of believing is a powerful force. I am reminded of a story from a pastor, about his daughter, Melodye Jan. The little girl, who was five at the time, asked her father for a doll house. He nodded yes, that he would build her one, and went back to reading his book. A while later, he glanced up from his reading to notice a backyard scene in which his daughter's arms were filled with dishes, toys, and dolls. She had begun amassing an enormous pile of playthings on the lawn. He asked his wife what the little girl was doing.

"Oh, you promised to build her a doll house, and she believes you. She's just getting ready for it."[4]

How marvelous would it be if our own faith were always so unjaded and pure? It is from that spirit that children are able to approach God with confidence and assuredness, asking Him bold questions and, I might add, also offering suggestions.

Here are some of my favorites, as recorded by Stuart Hample in the book, *Children's Letters to God*:

> *"Dear Mr. God, I wish you would not make it so easy for people to come apart. I had 3 stitches and a shot."* —Janet

> *"Please send me a pony. I never ask for anything before you can look it up."* —Bruce

> *"Dear God, Please send Dennis Clark to a different camp this year."* —Peter

> *"Dear God, Maybe Cain and Abel would not kill each other so much if they had their own rooms. It works with my brother."* —Larry

> *"Dear God, If you watch in church on Sunday I will show you my new shoes."* —Mickey

> *"Dear God, I don't ever feel alone since I found out about you."* —Nora[5]

It is fun to look at the perspective of children. Their easygoing nature—what some would call unfettered naiveté—make faith seem so simple. God has told us that we are to have a faith such as that of a child. Could it be that He desires all of us to exhibit the candid honesty we see in children?

The faith of children may seem simple. Perhaps too simple. But we should not be too quick to look down on the prayers of children, for they are certainly heard by God, and they can teach us much. I think an anecdote from Howard Hendricks does a good job of showing how the faith of a child is not as simple as it appears on the surface.

My children have taught me many things about theology. When they were quite young, we had a scholar visiting our home. After our meal, we were ready for our customary time of family worship, and we invited the man to join us. When it came time to pray, the kids, in typical childlike fashion, thanked Jesus for the tricycle and the sandbox and the fence and so on. Our guest could scarcely wait to take me aside.

"Professor Hendricks," he began, very much the lecturer that he was, "you don't mean to tell me that you're a professor in a theological seminary and yet you teach your children to pray for things like that?"

"I certainly do," I replied. "Do you ever pray about your Ford?" I knew he did. He had to: he was riding mostly on faith and frayed fabric!

"Of course," he replied, "but that's different."

"Oh really?" I countered. "What makes you think your

Ford is more important to God than my boy's tricycle?" Then I pressed him further. "You're on the road a lot. Do you ever pray for protection?"

"Brother Hendricks, I never go anywhere but that I pray for the Lord's journeying mercies."

"Well, safety is essentially what my boy is thanking Jesus for when he thanks him for the fence. That fence keeps out those great big dogs on the other side!"[6]

The faith of a child is simple, pure, and honest. But because Adulthood has a way of complicating so many things, that sort of faith is not always so simple for us grown-ups. In their book, *Putting the One Minute Manager to Work*, Kenneth Blanchard and Robert Lorber share a simple parable that perfectly illustrates how tricky faith can be...

A man slipped and fell off a cliff while hiking on a mountaintop. Luckily, he was able to grab a branch on the way down. Holding on for dear life, he looked down only to see a rock valley some fifteen hundred feet below. When he looked up, he saw that it was twenty feet to the cliff from which he had fallen. Panicked, he yelled, "Help! Help! Is anybody there? Help!"

A booming voice spoke up, "I am here, and I will save you if you believe in me."

"I believe! I believe!" yelled the man.

"If you believe in me, let go of the branch and I will save you."

The young man, hearing this, looked down again. Seeing

the rock valley below, he quickly looked back up and shouted, "Is there anybody else up there?"[7]

Faith is certainly not easy. The Bible says that faith is "the substance of things hoped for, the evidence of things not seen." (Hebrews 1:11) That is all well and good, but I don't know too many people who would put much stock in the lawyer whose case depended entirely on invisible evidence. In my own life, I have often lamented that it would be a lot easier to trust God if he gave me a better idea of what to expect. In those times, a lyric to a song by a group called Smalltown Poets usually comes to mind, "If you gave me a vision, would I never have reason to use my faith?"

We can be comforted in knowing that we don't need a huge faith in order to see real progress. In fact, it is said that if we had faith even as small as a tiny mustard seed, we would experience incredible results. Faith may not be easy, but the benefits can be remarkable. I'm not sure if I know of two more trusting and faith-filled people than my in-laws. Not only did they do a pretty good job of raising my wife, but they taught her (and me) a lot about having faith. Gary, my father-in-law, developed severe rheumatoid arthritis in his twenties. In subsequent years, the disease has ravaged his body, requiring the replacement of enough joints to make

> We can be comforted in knowing that we don't need a huge faith in order to see real progress.

a plumber tired. I'm pretty sure he's almost always in pain. I say "pretty sure" because you'd never know it. He's not one to complain.

Not surprisingly, Gary's condition racked up a slew of medical bills over the years. It was not uncommon for him to be out of work for months recuperating from some surgery. One time I asked my in-laws how they were able to support four girls with their income fluctuating so wildly. They said that they tried to be responsible with what they had and trusted God to provide for their needs. It seemed too simple. But they told me of a time when Gary had to get his hip replaced. He would be laid up for months. They had a little bit saved up, but not enough to make the house payments and raise four girls. All they had was their faith that God would take care of them.

Shortly after the surgery, when Gary had returned home, a co-worker named Phil called, wondering if he could stop by to say hi. He spent some time watching football, and they chatted about how things were going on the job. When Phil got up to leave, he handed Joyce an envelope filled with wrinkled, dirty dollar bills that smelled of cigar smoke.

Four hundred of them.

He had taken up a collection from the 400 men on the job, who agreed that a dollar was the least they could do for one of their brothers. Gary and Joyce were floored by the generosity, and very grateful. What they didn't know was that Phil would be by almost every week for the next few months with another envelope. By the time Gary was healed and ready to get back in the workforce, the contributions had amounted to over $6,000. Indeed, God had rewarded their faith.

I can also relate to the faithfulness of God to provide the light that dispels any monstrous fears I may have. When you break from convention and start your own business, it doesn't take long for you to wonder if you're certifiably crazy. You wonder, were all those people who encouraged you to go for it (if you were lucky to have any of those) just being nice but never thought you'd go through with it? You wonder if you have what it takes, if you're good enough, or if you're just fooling yourself. I have prayed many prayers asking for God to turn this train around if I was doing the wrong thing. So far He hasn't, and I have often depended on the faith that I must be headed in the right direction or God wouldn't have let me go this far. After all, your parents may let you go off in your own direction in the backyard, but not if your backyard is the Amazon Rainforest.

In the Bible, God says, "For I know the plans I have for you. Plans to prosper you and not harm you, plans to give you hope and a future." (Jeremiah 29:11) I use this verse to remind myself that God has things figured out, and His intention is not to abandon me in some dark alley.

Even with this faith, I only need to revisit some old journal entries to see some good examples of my faith freaking out. Looking back at some of the early days of my journaling, I am embarrassed by some of the fears I spent time worrying about. Most of them never materialized (there's that False Evidence Appearing Real concept again). The few that did were never to the degree of destruction that I had anticipated. Again, a lot of my concerns were financial. On each of the dozens of occasions when I wondered if we'd have enough cash flow to keep this company afloat, God has responded with a resounding "yes."

An order would come in, an opportunity would present itself, and lo and behold, we're still here.

So far, in the relatively short time I've been on Earth, I've found life to be a thrilling adventure, one with more uncertain turns than any roller coaster known to man. The world is a big place; sometimes even scary. By observing the easy faith of children, perhaps we can see that faith can offer us a release from the gnawing worries that press down on us daily. Will we make rent this month? Am I doomed to be involved in the next round of layoffs? How will we ever afford college? Do I have what it takes to be a good dad?

These questions, and many like them, loom large in our lives—even larger than the bloodthirsty creatures that lurked in the shadows of our childhood bedrooms. May we be ever mindful that there IS someone bigger than the questions, bigger than the monsters that keep us up at night. May we remember that we have a hand to hold through all the scariness that life dishes out, and it's a hand that will most certainly lead us to a safe place. And, in the darkest of nights, may we always count on that simple childlike faith to light our paths, keeping the monsters at bay better than any night-light ever could.

And the monsters will be forced to go wherever it is that monsters go.

11 TiPS   Have Faith

Sometimes I wonder about life.

1 Find a really good place to watch a sunset. Stay long enough to see the magnificent colors fade to black as the stars begin to peek out. It's hard not to have a great feeling of something bigger than you when you're in the midst of such awesome beauty.

2 If you're the praying type, pray earnestly for an increase in your faith. If you're not the praying type, or you're unsure about the whole "God thing," why not give it a try on your way to work sometime. Trust me, there's no right or wrong way to do it. If a three-year-old can do it, YOU can do it. Just give God a chance and he'll probably surprise you. Besides, what do you have to lose?

3 Ask friends you know who have a strong faith to go out for coffee. Ask them questions about their faith, and how they came to where they are now. You're likely to encounter honest answers and heartfelt stories that may surprise you.

4 Write down all of your fears, all of the things that keep you up at night. For each fear, write down the WORST thing you could possibly imagine coming of it. Then write down what is most LIKELY to come from it. Finally, write down the BEST possible scenario that could arise out of this thing you fear. Not only does this simple process give you a measure of peaceful perspective, but if you keep the list around and look back on it a year from now, you'll see what I mean when I say how most fears never materialize at all.

5 Think of all of the great things that have happened in your life. Did all of these things come about by pure chance, blind luck, or simple coincidence? Keep in mind that coincidence is just God's way of remaining anonymous.

6 Dust off a Bible and look up stories that talk about great faith. If you need a place to start, try the story of the three guys who were thrown into a furnace (Daniel 3:1-30), or the guy who God let walk on water (Matthew 14:22-33), or the person who was thrown into a den of hungry lions and lived to tell about it (Daniel 6:1-28).

7 Here's another trick that will help you deal with the unexpected and unpleasant little things that come out of nowhere to add extra levels of stress to your life. Ask yourself the question, "Will this matter five years from now?"

8 Check out www.DailyGuideposts.com/positivethinking. There you will find "Thought Conditioners" by Norman Vincent Peale. They are spiritual affirmations that you can repeat to yourself throughout the day, giving you a greater sense of peace and a deeper faith.

9 Add some inspirational music to your collection. There was a time when "gospel music" was boring, cheesy, and just not good. No more. There are artists in every genre who are on par with the quality of anything you listen to now. Want some recommendations? If you like Top 40 stuff, check out "Second Decade" by Michael W. Smith. If you're into a more adult alternative, Starbucks-type vibe, go with "Who We Are Instead" by Jars of Clay. If hip-hop and rap are your cup of tea, check out Toby-Mac.

10 Find a church to go to, somewhere friendly and welcoming. If you already belong to a church, make sure you're going there regularly. There is no better way to build up your faith than with a little spiritual nutrition.

11 If you're really adventurous, find a guided religious retreat organized through your local church. You're likely to find retreats for men, women, single people, and married people. A retreat I went on in college literally changed my life. I assure you, it will be well worth your time.

Maintain
Perspective

*"Life moves pretty fast. If you don't stop and look
around once in a while, you could miss it."*

Ferris Bueller

Kids have interesting tastes. Ever notice how they have the
peculiar tendency to want the same toy as every other kid
on the face of the planet? Never is it more evident than around
Christmastime. Parents go ballistic trying to find the magical,
market-driven, toy du jour that every child has been asking
for since the trees started getting naked. I've seen many of
these trends in my own lifetime. The most remarkable one I

can remember during my own childhood was sometime in the early eighties, long before Pokemon became a household name or Elmo was ever tickled. I'm thinking of the time when the Cabbage Patch craze swept the nation. I'm sure I'm too young to really even remember the specifics, but I've heard many stories of desperate parents searching high and low for the chubby little dolls with autographed bums.[1]

On one proud Christmas, my brother and I were the privileged adopters of Timothy Sylvester and Avery Wendell. Honestly, I don't recall ever asking for a Cabbage Patch Kid, as my preoccupation revolved more around *Star Wars* figures. However, I remember being surprised by the gift. I suspect my parents were affected by the media hysteria, and had probably run across a great deal on the pair of yarn-headed babies.[2]

Since then, I've lived through many other such frenetic fads, and anticipate many, many more. Sometimes I wonder who really drives the holiday season scavenger hunt for the coolest new thing. Is it the kids, or their parents?

I've seen more and more parents working longer and longer hours, trying to compensate for their lack of involvement in their children's lives with "stuff." Expensive, trendy, hard-to-find stuff. Kids certainly love toys, but I doubt I could find one child who would really rather have some electronic video game than an afternoon out with Dad in the park. Kids seem to have an innate perspective on what's important in life. Mark Twain once said, "We are always too busy for our children; we never give them the time or interest they deserve. We lavish gifts upon them; but the most precious gift, our personal association, which means so much to them, we give grudgingly."

My nephew Andrew can be as self-absorbed as any four-year-old, but he also exhibits an inborn sense of perspective. When his mom was pregnant with his second sibling, she carried the baby-sister-to-be full term, and then some. One night, after the targeted due date, she finally went into labor. Of course it happened in the middle of the night, and chaos ensued as the two boys were rushed off to a babysitter's while Mom and Dad sped to the hospital. After a valiant effort, the labor process just...stopped. Apparently, little Grace was experiencing cold feet. The doctor sent Mom home to rest and wait. Of course, the hard part was picking up the boys, who were expecting to greet a new brother or sister. Disappointment and emotions ran high, and tears came from all directions. Seeing his mother cry, Andrew wiped his own tears and said thoughtfully, "Mom, don't cry. It'll be okay; the baby will come out soon."

> I doubt I could find one child who would really rather have some electronic video game than an afternoon out with Dad in the park.

Children just seem to have an otherworldly wisdom that helps them keep focused on the present. They embrace life as it comes. Perhaps it's easy not to get caught up in the past when you have so little of it, or not to be worried about days far in the future when tomorrow seems an eternity away (especially when tomorrow is your birthday). But there is power in the present moment. As of this writing, Kim and I don't have children of our own, but I am looking forward to fatherhood. I have all kinds of plans in my head to make sure I can put these lessons to good use. I want to be a great dad; I want to spend lots and lots of quality time with my kids. I have already planned out "date nights." My idea is to take one night a month and spend it with each of my children. If I have a boy, it'll be a guys' night out. Maybe we'll grab pizza and go to a ball game. With a girl, it'll be "date-night." We won't always go to extravagant places, but she'll always be treated like a princess. Even though I don't have any kids, I know how fast they grow up, and my window of opportunity for doing these things (before they consider me a nerd and are embarrassed to be seen with me) is a short one. But hopefully I will be able to give them some good memories while celebrating the importance of proper perspective.

National surveys show that parents spend 40 percent less time with their children than they did 30 years ago. Some of the blame goes to an increasing emphasis on self-fulfillment and materialism. But even for well-intentioned parents, the challenge of carving out quality time with the family is a difficult one. How do we fit everything in?

At an industry meeting, Stephen Covey, an expert in time management, was speaking to executives. To drive home a point, he used an illustration those executives would never forget. As this man stood in front of the group of high-powered overachievers, he said, "Okay, time for a quiz." Then he pulled out a one-gallon, wide-mouthed Mason jar and set it on a table in front of him. He produced about a dozen fist-sized rocks and carefully placed them, one at a time, into the jar. When the jar was filled to the top and no more rocks would fit inside, he asked, "Is this jar full?"

Everyone in the class said, "Yes."

Then he asked, "Really?" He reached under the table and pulled out a bucket of gravel. He dumped some gravel in and shook the jar, causing pieces of gravel to work themselves down into the spaces between the big rocks. Then he asked the group once more, "Is the jar full?"

By this time the class was onto him. "Probably not," one of them answered.

"Good!" he replied. He reached under the table and brought out a bucket of sand. He started dumping the sand in and it went into all the spaces left between the rocks and the gravel. Once more he asked the question, "Is this jar full?"

"No!" the class shouted.

Once again he said, "Good!" Then he grabbed a pitcher of water and began to pour it in until the jar was filled to the brim. Then he looked up at the class and asked, "What is the point of this illustration?"

One woman raised her hand and said, "The point is, no matter how full your schedule is, if you try really hard, you can always fit some more things into it!"

"No," the speaker replied, "That's not the point. The truth this illustration teaches is: If you don't put the big rocks in first, you'll never get them in at all."[3]

"Don't forget until too late that the business of life is not business, but living," said   B.C. Forbes, founder of *Forbes* magazine. It has been said countless times, but it is true every time: No one on their deathbed ever wishes they had spent more time at the office. The growing-up process throws a lot of things at us; before you know it, you forget what the "big rocks" are. You'll do fine if you just keep in mind that, as I stated at the beginning of this book, the important things in life aren't things. Things have a nasty habit of staying behind when our time on earth is up. As Denis Waitly eloquently said, "Happiness cannot be traveled to, owned, earned, worn, or consumed. Happiness is the spiritual experience of living every minute with love, grace, and gratitude."

Kids teach us that the things to be valued are smiles, hugs, laughter, and shared time with the people you love. One of the biggest reasons kids love being read to is not because they desperately want to hear *Green Eggs and Ham* for the one millionth time, but because they crave and delight in the shared experience.

> Kids teach us that the things to be valued are smiles, hugs, laughter, and shared time with the people you love.

The terrorist attack of September 11, 2001 was a horrific period in America's history. But somehow, out of the ashen darkness, an uplifting spirit of cooperation, compassion, and prayer swept through the country. It was a tragic wake-up call that stirred our senses to what is really important in life. People donated blood in record numbers. Heartfelt prayers were taken up by the wind that swept the flags. Everybody hugged their loved ones just a little tighter.

President George W. Bush is admired for how he led our nation through that difficult period. His optimism and compassionate perspective saw its beginnings in his own childhood. Author Stephen Mansfield describes how a young George W. Bush was able to bring light to his own mother after a devastating family tragedy. After George's sister Robin died from leukemia when he was seven, a deep sadness crept into the Bush home. George took it upon himself to try to cheer his mother up with jokes and stories—anything to get a smile. On one occasion, his mother overheard him tell a neighbor child that he could not play because his mother needed him. That comment helped start the healing process in Barbara, who received a lesson in perspective from her thoughtful little boy.[4]

Kim and I have been abundantly blessed through our work with The Make-A-Wish Foundation, which grants the wishes of children with life-threatening medical conditions.[5] One of the most valuable lessons I've taken from my experience is the importance of living in the present and appreciating what you've got. Kim and I are "Wish Granters." The title is a bit misleading, however. We are not footing the bill for Disney vacations, or even planning them for that matter. Dedicated people do the real work—people who rarely get to see the kids whose wishes they're striving to fulfill. They're busy booking flights, making arrangements, and generally making dreams come true. What Kim and I do is meet with the wish kids and their families to find out what their wishes are. For this, we get a disproportionate amount of the credit.

I remember meeting our fifth wish kid and his parents. It was heartbreaking in the truest sense of the word. This only child had been born with a severe, super-rare heart defect. He'd had over a dozen heart surgeries, and was only five years old—the same age as the kindergartners who run around Kim's classroom with carefree spirits and socks wet from the snow. The fact that he was five was a miracle. He wasn't have supposed to live beyond three days old. The little guy had made more comebacks than Brett Favre, but his heart was giving out, and his chance for a transplant grew slimmer every day. How many five-year-old organ donors are out there, I couldn't help but wonder. Not many, I was assured.

Speechless was the only word I can use to describe myself that night. I know better than to try and "fix" things with words that do little more than shine a spotlight on my own ignorance. What do you say to parents who are openly sharing the details of their son's dangerous surgeries, endless emergency room visits and lengthy med schedule? How do you not break down in tears when you watch a video of birthday highlights, knowing full well that the little boy, hooked up to a maze of tubes and yet happily munching on popcorn, may not have more celebrations to add to the highlight reel? What's the right thing to say when the boy's tough security-guard father explains how often he cries and how hard it is to see his only son deteriorate a little more every day? And what words are appropriate when you hear that his three wishes are 1) a new heart from Jesus, 2) the chance to play with other kids, and 3) to go to Disney World and meet Buzz Lightyear?

Nothing. There is nothing you can say. Not "Sorry." Not "God has a plan." Not "Be grateful for the time you've had with him." Not "I'm sure he'll get a heart." Nothing. I figured all I could do was listen. So I did the best I could. Talk about feeling inadequate.

The more we talked about the trip to Disney World, however, the more excited we all got. He'd get to fly on a plane, be around other kids, be treated like a king, and hopefully get to meet his hero, Mr. Lightyear. I knew that it would be an experience that the entire family would cherish forever. And one they would never be able to afford on their own. World-renowned heart surgeons don't come cheap, after all.

Afterward, I wondered why they were so open with everything. I mean, who were we? Total strangers. Two kids who didn't know jack. I guess maybe they could tell we cared. Kim pointed out that they probably were also hoping to show us that their son was worthy of this wish that they were all so excited about. Worthy? Kim and I have a hard time accepting gifts from people, so I could see her point, but I couldn't help but think how ridiculous that sounded—who could possibly be *more* worthy?

On the drive home, I questioned my sanity. Why would I willingly put myself into a situation like this: allowing myself to get emotionally involved with people I'd never met, standing face to face with the questions that have no answers? I concluded that it certainly would be easier to count my lucky stars, pretending that things like this don't really happen, and that, if they do, they'll never happen to me. Isn't that what most people do?

All I know is that we got involved in this because of where God has led us with *Kim & Jason*. And I get the sense that this is just the tip of the iceberg. Every day I understand a little bit more what I guess I've always known...when you commit yourself to God's plan for your life, you can expect the scariest, most difficult, but incredibly fulfilling and rewarding journey you could ever imagine. As I go along, I somehow seem to be more at peace and have more questions at the same time. When I think of this little kid, and hear the stories of how many lives he's literally changed, I can see God working. I can see a glimpse of His plan. But I still question it. Why him? Why this way?

I think of birds, and how confused they would be if they tried to comprehend the mind of man. It would be impossible. I guess that's how it is for us. We get pieces, but our perspective just isn't big enough to see the whole thing. And so we're left with the questions. Questions that have no answers.

> Appreciate what time you've been given. Cherish your family. Pay attention to what's important.

At least not ones we'll get in this life. But I've been fortunate to receive these lessons from my Make-A-Wish experiences: Appreciate what time you've been given. Cherish your family. Pay attention to what's important.

In the book *Dream a New Dream*, Dale Galloway tells a touching story about a child's ability to be steadfastly and selflessly focused on what's important in a wonderfully told story called "Valentines":

Little Chad was a shy, quiet young fella. One day he came home and told his mother he'd like to make a valentine for everyone in his class. Her heart sank. She thought, I wish he wouldn't do that! Because she had watched the children when they walked home from school. Her Chad was always behind them. They laughed and hung on to each other and talked to each other. But Chad was never included. Nevertheless, she decided she would go along with her son. So she purchased the paper and glue and crayons. For three whole weeks, night after night, Chad painstakingly made thirty-five valentines.

Valentine's Day dawned, and Chad was beside himself with excitement! He carefully stacked them up, put them in a bag, and bolted out the door. His mom decided to bake him his favorite cookies and serve them up warm and nice with a cool glass of milk when he came home from school. She just knew he would be disappointed...maybe that would ease the pain a little. It hurt her to think that he wouldn't get many valentines—maybe none at all.

That afternoon she had the cookies and milk on the table. When she heard the children outside she looked out the window. Sure enough here they came, laughing and having the best time. And, as always, there was Chad in the rear. He walked a little faster than usual. She fully expected him to burst into tears as soon as he got inside. His arms were empty, she noticed, and when the door opened she choked back the tears.

"Mommy has some warm cookies and milk for you."

But he hardly heard her words. He just marched right on

by, his face aglow, and all he could say was: "Not a one…not a one."

And then he added, "I didn't forget one, not a single one!"[6]

Children possess such a wonderful combination of compassion, sincerity, and selflessness. During one school year, Kim had a student who had Russell Silver Syndrome, which contributed to serious developmental problems. The little girl wore hearing aids and had to be fed through a feeding tube in her stomach.

Amazingly to me, her classmates intuitively rallied around her, took her under their wing and looked out for her.

At recess, as kids scrambled out the doors to freedom, Sarah had trouble keeping up with the herd of excited children. But there would always be a handful of classmates who would grab her arm and head out to the playground with her, at her pace. There was more than one occasion when Sarah's hearing aids came out of place, and friends, modeling what they had seen adults do, did their best to fix the situation.

Sarah's feeding routine involved a technique called "venting," which had to be performed every day by people on staff. The only time staff was available to perform the 15 to 20 minute process was during the regularly scheduled (and much cherished) playtime. While the staff was working, Sarah was left sidelined, sitting at a table. Her friends took it upon themselves to bring playtime to Sarah. Every single day, without fail, they would sit at the table with her, playing games in which she could participate. Time and time again, the kids saw past the superficial differences to the value of Sarah as a person. Their compassionate nature helped her have a very successful and happy first year of school.

Here is another story that reminds me that children have a perspective beyond our own imaginations. A perspective that allows them to see things we cannot see. A perspective that we would be blessed to share.

A mother brought a crippled boy with a hunched back into her home as a companion for her own son. She warned her son to be very careful not to refer to the other boy's deformity, since this was a sensitive matter to him. And she encouraged him to play with his new friend as if he were a normal child. But after listening to her son play with him for a few minutes, she heard him ask his companion, "Do you know what that is on your back?" The crippled boy was embarrassed, hesitated a moment, but before he could respond, his friend answered the question for him by saying, "It is the box that holds your wings, and someday God is going to break it open, and you will fly away to be an angel." [7]

By tapping into our own childlike spirit, we too will be able to see what is unseen. The cobwebs will be cleared and we'll be able to tell between the truth and the lies, able to embrace the things that are really important.

When it comes down to it, we only get one life. Let's not miss it. No one is guaranteed tomorrow. Life is too short to get caught up in trivialities and superficialities, worries and regret, fleeting fads and fashions. A selection from a fellow named Brother Jeremiah perfectly summarizes the childlike spirit. If the outcome of writing this book is only to gain a wider audience for his wise words, I shall be satisfied.

If I had my life to live over again, I'd try to make more mistakes next time. I would relax. I would limber up. I would be sillier than I have been on this trip. I know of a very few things I would take seriously. I would take more trips. I would climb more mountains, swim more rivers and watch more sunsets. I would do more walking and looking. I would eat more ice cream and fewer beans. I would have more actual troubles and fewer imaginary ones. You see, I am one of those people who lives prophylactically and sensibly and sanely, hour after hour, day after day. Oh, I've had my moments; and if I had it to do over again, I'd have more of them. In fact, I'd try to have nothing else. Just moments, one after another, instead of living so many years ahead each day. I have been one of those people who never go anywhere without a thermometer, a hot water bottle, a gargle, a raincoat, aspirin and a parachute. If I had to do it over again, I would go places, do things, and travel lighter than I have.

If I had my life to live over, I would ride on merry-go-rounds, and pick more daisies.[8]

11 TiPS Maintain Perspective

1 Kids don't care as much about material things as we think they do. If you have children, or are close to some nieces or nephews, make it a priority to spend some time with them. Nothing fancy, just "be." Read a story, go to the park, play catch. The memories you create will be worth more than any new toy.

2 If you're looking for a creative and heartfelt gift idea, consider making a memory jar. Kim and I made them for our parents one year for Christmas. Just get some construction paper and cut it into little strips. On each strip, write a cherished memory or story about the person. Fold the strips and put them in a cool jar. When you give the gift, instruct the person to pull out and read one memory each day. You would be hard-pressed to find a better gift at any price.

3 Start a gratitude journal. Get a journal or notebook with lined pages. Each day, maybe at night before you go to sleep, list five things you are grateful for. The list can contain simple things, like gratitude for chocolate, or more complex things, such as a successful surgery.

After only a month or two, as you focus on abundance, you will be amazed at how your perspective on life has changed.

4 If you celebrate Christmas, try going caroling. It's a lost art, but with a small or large group of friends, the benefits are huge. It's hard to describe the feeling of peace you get bringing a bit of joy to unsuspecting people during a busy time of year. Admittedly, I'm a little biased, because I met my wife Christmas caroling.

5 Get involved with a local charity or church. If you like kids, seek out some children's charity, like Big Brothers Big Sisters or The Make-A-Wish Foundation. If you enjoy spending time with seniors, volunteer some time at a nearby nursing home. I promise you, the few hours you give up will change your life and your perspective.

6 Quit procrastinating. The next day you're stuck inside because of the weather, pull out all of those old photos and start putting them in albums. If you're exceptionally crafty, put together a scrapbook, adding a few pages here and there. It takes time, but you will never regret the effort spent organizing your memories.

7 A good way to get a deeper sense of perspective is to spend time with people who have been around longer than you have. Make it a point to ask your parents, or better yet, your grandparents, what it was like growing up. How did they fall in love? What did they do when they were kids? It's easy to get caught up in the here and now, but a little history can go a long way.

8 Do you have some sort of memory box for preserving random things like ticket stubs, old mementos, photos, and special knickknacks? Why not? It doesn't even have to be organized, just one centralized place to go for a little pick-me-up when you're down in the dumps.

9 Write a letter of gratitude to someone you care about. Tell that person how much he or she means to you. Better yet, if you're really ambitious, create a handmade card. Use plenty of glitter.

10 Visit someplace new. Even if you can't afford an expensive European vacation, you can plan a short day trip, or maybe a long weekend. Just go somewhere you've never been, and see things you've never seen. Your battery will get recharged, and your life will be made richer by regular trips outside of your familiar surroundings.

11 The next time you see kids running a lemonade stand, buy a glass, and leave them a really big tip. It will make your day, and probably their week.

Conclusion

*"So, like a forgotten fire, a childhood can
always flare up again within us."*

Gaston Bachelard

Well, that's it. Eight little secrets that hopefully aren't so
secret anymore. Eight little antidotes guaranteed to cure
even the worst case of Adultitis.

I hope that somewhere, in my struggle to find the right
words, you've been touched by the truth of the power inside
you. The power of childhood. I hope you have come to believe,
as I have, that by appreciating the little things, you can break

free from the monotony and boredom of adulthood. By daring to dream big, you can truly accomplish things that you never thought possible. And with a little bit of curiosity, you'll be well on your way to new opportunities to change unfavorable conditions and solve seemingly unsolvable problems. Your passion can make even the most mundane chores fun and interesting and lead you to a more productive home and work life. By taking time to play, you'll improve your health by melting away built-up stress and fatigue. A commitment to honesty will lead you to be respected by friends and colleagues, and an increase in faith will ease your mind about the things you worry about most. Finally, I hope you have been encouraged to maintain perspective in life, so that you can make the most out of every minute you've been given.

Whether your childhood is filled with fond memories, or something you'd just as soon forget, always be mindful that it's never too late to have a second childhood, one that's even better than the first. I encourage you to take some of the ideas in this book and try them out. You might be a little rusty, but don't give up.

There is a child inside you who can't wait to run free, who is eager to stomp through puddles, believe in fairy tales, and live life with reckless abandon.

And make angels in the snow.

Endnotes

Here begins the parade of endnotes. Some are straightforward bibliographic notes, some are helpful web sites and books you may want to visit, and the rest are mildly interesting asides that didn't make it into the main text. Enjoy.

INTRODUCTION.

1 **one of my gifts:** For those of you who get the whole "it's a gift" thing and are wondering how I get my ideas from a purely technical side, here goes: Early on in the week, I go somewhere to generate ideas (usually a Barnes & Noble or a Starbucks, although I don't care for coffee). My goal is to get seven days worth of material. I sit for a few hours coming up with situations to put the characters in, and usually, they dictate how events unfold. I try to come up with around fourteen gags. Then, I let the ol' subconscious stew. At the end of the week, I take another few hours and review my ideas. Sometimes I am amazed by how lame some of the ideas are (which is why I come up with more gags than I'll need). If I laugh out loud, I know I have a keeper. I pick the seven best jokes, fine-tune the writing, and do thumbnail sketches in a notebook. This serves as a guide when I draw up the strips a few weeks later.

2 **never enter it:** Matthew 18:15-17.

3 **in our ear:** Also, don't dump pumpkin seeds down the drain. The janitor at my wife's school had to dismantle quite a bit of plumbing to remove a baby pumpkin that had begun growing under the sink in her kindergarten classroom.

DELIGHT IN THE LITTLE THINGS.

1 **share a bag of fries:** Looking back, many of the toys that accompanied Happy Meals back then now command a pretty penny on eBay. I would comment on the big opportunity my mom missed in her frugality, but I cannot say with certainty that the toys would have made it to my adulthood in mint condition. Unless mint condition means dirt-caked from being buried in the backyard.

2 **Make-A-Wish Foundation®:** An awesome organization that grants the wishes of children with life-threatening medical conditions, enriching the human experience with hope, strength, and joy. Children over the age of 2 1/2, and under the age of 18 at the time of referral, who have life-threatening medical conditions, are eligible for a wish. The Make-A-Wish Foundation accepts referrals for potential wish children from parents or guardians of the child, medical professionals, or the children themselves. If you know a child who might qualify for a wish, please contact your local Make-A-Wish chapter. http://www.wish.org

3 **earwax and earthworms:** Jelly Belly® released *Harry Potter* inspired Bertie Bott's Every Flavor Beans with such mouth-watering flavors as earwax and earthworm, as well as soap, spaghetti, and, yes, vomit.
http://www.jellybelly.com

4 **certain little comic strip:** In case you haven't been paying attention, that would be *Kim & Jason*, which you can read at:
http://www.KimandJason.com

5 **another story:** Yes, it's true. I have a hard time showing the unbridled enthusiasm that my wife and mother think I should.

Just because I don't jump up and down and spit out quarters doesn't mean I'm not appreciative. I guess it's not really much of a story, but more of a warning should you ever decide to get me something very nice.

6 **green worm:** This story was first shared on my blog, "Bird Droppings." "Bird" comes from J-Bird, the nickname my father bestowed on me. "Droppings" comes from my attempt at being clever. You can read it here: http://www.KimandJason.com/blog

DREAM BIG.

1 **the townsfolk saying:** Why don't we refer to people as townsfolk any more?

2 **nothing was impossible:** I used these memories of me saving the world to create the Super J character that Jason turns into from time to time in my comic strip. He's a fun character to write for, partially because of the brash, albeit misguided, confidence that can overwhelm a person when he slips on some superhero Underoos®.

3 **Norman Vincent Peale:** If you haven't already, read *The Power of Positive Thinking* by Norman Vincent Peale. It went a long way in helping me to see just how much difference can be made by a simple change of attitude.

4 **suddenly attainable:** Another book to check out is *Simple Steps to Impossible Dreams* by Steven K. Scott. With stories, advice, and plenty of interactive material to help you create your own personal plan, Scott gives you the step-by-step directions to fulfill your dreams.

---

5 **testing your aim:** Glenn Van Ekeren, *Speaker's Sourcebook II* (New York: Prentice Hall Press, 1994), 110-111.

GET CURIOUS.

1 **outside of his tights:** Crazythoughts.com, 24 Aug. 2004 http://www.crazythoughts.com.

2 **personal touch inside:** Happily, Kim & Jason greeting cards are available, in exchange for money, online at The Kim & Jason Lemonade Stand and offline at various places that sell greeting cards. http://www.KimandJason.com/lemonade_stand

3 **the word "why":** Jacqui Sakowski is available for hire as an experienced consultant who will help you boost your salesmanship. She is passionate, professional, and a lot of fun. http://www.sakowskiconsulting.com

4 **holy curiosity:** Here are some more "why?" questions to heighten your curiosity...

- Why do people feel compelled to touch surfaces that have "wet paint" signs on them?
- Why do we call it a "hamburger" when there is no ham in it?
- Why do they call it a "near miss" when two airplanes almost collide? Wouldn't "near hit" be a better phrase?
- Why do banks charge a "non-sufficient funds" fee on money they already know we do not have?
- Why do we drive on a parkway and park on a driveway?
- Why are they called "apartments" when they are stuck together?

- Why isn't the whole airplane made out of the material used to build the indestructible black box?
- Why is it we think there has to be an answer to every question?
- If Christianity offered full and final answers to every question, we would not call it a "faith."

LIVE PASSIONATELY.

1 **like more playing:** The song we sang was not entirely made up. I think we borrowed it from Sesame Street or the Electric Company or something. The chorus, which we repeated over and over, was, "Co-op-er-a-tion is the answer."

2 **helped Elvis Presley become successful:** Elvis Presley was a small-time artist who recorded a handful of obscure songs such as "Hound Dog" and "Jailhouse Rock." He caused quite a stir when he shook his hips on *The Ed Sullivan Show*. He passed away in 1977. Allegedly.

3 **pinpoint our passion:** A very helpful tool for uncovering your true passion and developing your life's mission statement is a book called *The Path*, by Laurie Beth Jones. I read it my senior year in college and it (quite literally) shaped the direction my life has taken.

4 **MADD:** Janice Lord, "Really MADD: Looking Back at 20 Years," *Driven,* Spring 2000.

PLAY.

1 **the first step:** Admitting you have a problem *is* the first step in treating playaholism. Some warning signs include taking toys with you to bed, begging for loose change to purchase trinkets from those little machines they have in the front of supermarkets, and insisting on drinking only from straws that look like an on-ramp designed by indecisive engineers.

2 **emotional, and physical:** Alliance For Childhood, "Play Fact Sheet,", 2 June 2004 <http://www.allianceforchildhood.net/projects/play//pdf_files/play_fact_sheet.pdf>.

3 **happiness in adulthood:** Edward Hallowell, *The Childhood Roots of Adult Happiness*, New York: Ballantine, 2002.

4 **the rinse cycle that got him:** Robert J. Morgan, *Nelson's Complete Book of Stories, Illustrations, & Quotes* (Nashville: Thomas Nelson, Inc., 2000), 716.

5 **complaints or disorders:** http://www.stress.org

6 **fair measure of play:** The Institute For Play, "The Importance of Play", 2 June 2004 <http://www.instituteforplay.com/5importance_of_play.htm>.

7 **can't do it in twelve:** Clifton Fadiman and Andre Bernard, eds. *Bartlett's Book of Anecdotes* (Boston: Little, Brown and Company, 2000), 75.

8 **Sales Servants:** We call sales representatives who work for my company "Sales Servants." It serves as a reminder that a good sales rep is always mindful of trying to find the best solution for the customer and puts the customer's needs first. We have found that when a sales rep has that mindset, it's usually a win-win for everyone involved.

BE HONEST.

1 **...never:** What, am I the only one who detests Candyland®? As Stinky (the stuffed skunk that co-stars in *Kim & Jason*) once said, "I find it slightly implausible that anyone could play Candyland all day long without giving in to the uncontrollable urge to foam at the mouth, jump through a window, and run directly into oncoming traffic."

2 **examples lived before them:** Allan C. Emery, *A Turtle on a Fencepost* (Waco: Word Books, 1979), 31.

3 **guilty my whole life:** "New York Cabbie Teaches Honesty to Children," *Reuters [New York]* 1998.

4 **quickly returned:** Stephen Mansfield, *The Faith of George W. Bush* (New York: Tarcher/Penguin, 2003), 28.

5 **buy from them:** Glenn Van Ekeren, *Speaker's Sourcebook II* (New York: Prentice Hall Press, 1994), 194.

6 **don't have to remember:** Glenn Van Ekeren, *Speaker's Sourcebook II* (New York: Prentice Hall Press, 1994), 195.

7 **that's my religion:** Adam Khan, *Self-Help Stuff That Works* (Bellevue: YouMe Works, 1999), 17.

8 **nothing to hide:** Clifton Fadiman and Andre Bernard, eds. *Bartlett's Book of Anecdotes* (Boston: Little, Brown and Company, 2000), 124.

HAVE FAITH.

1 **drift off into dreamland:** Fire trucks freaked me out, but somehow, a life-size poster of a ferocious Lou Ferrigno as The Incredible Hulk didn't faze me.

2 **before I came here:** Mary Ann Casler and Tona Pearce Myers, eds. Butterfly Kisses (Novato, California: New World Library, 2001).

3 **good to be alive:** I feel I should clarify that I don't actually hold my hand out while I'm walking like that. Usually.

4 **ready for it:** John Bisango, *The Power of Positive Praying* (Grand Rapids, MI: Zondervan, 1965).

5 **found out about you:** Stuart Hample and Eric Marshall, *Children's Letters To God* (New York: Workman Publishing, 1991).

6 **dogs on the other side:** Howard Hendricks, *Standing Together* (Gresham, Oregon: Vision House Publishing, Inc., 1995).

7 **anybody else up there?:** Kenneth Blanchard and Robert Lorber, *Putting the One Minute Manager to Work* (New York: Berkley Books, 1985), 20.

MAINTAIN PERSPECTIVE.

1 **autographed bums:** I seem to recall that they also smelled like baby powder, but maybe that was because I sprinkled baby powder on mine every chance I got.

2 **yarn-headed babies:** If you're interested in revisiting some fads of the past, check out the Time Capsule on KimandJason.com. It's got a year-by-year look at some of the popular toys, TV shows, and movies of your childhood. Plus you can find out how much a dozen eggs cost when you were born.

3 **never get them in at all:** Stephen Covey, *First Things First* (New York: Fireside, 1994).

----

4 **thoughtful little boy:** Stephen Mansfield, *The Faith of George W. Bush* (New York: Tarcher/Penguin, 2003), 33.

5 **medical conditions:** Just a repeat from earlier in the book... Make-A-Wish is an awesome organization that grants the wishes of children with life-threatening medical conditions enriching the human experience with hope, strength, and joy. Children over the age of 2 1/2, and under the age of 18 at the time of referral, who have a life-threatening medical condition, are eligible for a wish. The Make-A-Wish Foundation accepts referrals for potential wish children from parents or guardians of the child, medical professionals, or the children themselves. If you know a child who might qualify for a wish, please contact your local Make-A-Wish chapter.

http://www.wish.org

6 **not a single one:** "Valentines" by Dale Galloway, *Dream A New Dream* (Carol Stream, Illinois: Tyndale House Publishers, Inc., 1975).

7 **to be an angel:** L.B. Cowman, *Streams in the Desert* (Grand Rapids, Michigan: Zondervan Publishing House, 1997), 448.

8 **pick more daisies:** "If I Had My Life To Live Over" by Brother Jeremiah. Source unknown. Quoted from *Fresh Elastic For Stretched Out Moms* (Fleming H. Revell, 1986).

# # #

About the Author

Photo Credit: Beau Meyer

Jason Kotecki, known as The Champion of Childhood, is an engaging speaker, entertaining author, and creator of the internationally known comic strip, *Kim & Jason*. He is widely regarded as an expert in helping people to "escape adulthood" and "return to childhood." His mission is to inspire, entertain, and encourage others to renew their childlike faith and believe in their dreams. He met his wife Kim way back in 1995. It wasn't long before the two realized they shared a kindred childlike spirit. One day, Jason sketched himself and his girlfriend as young cartoon characters, and they began appearing on all kinds of homemade (cheap) cards and gifts designed to win her heart. Jason's efforts were not in vain, as the couple was married in May 2000. Since then, the characters have taken on lives and personalities of their own and the "real" Kim and Jason have built a company (JBiRD iNK) to promote and distribute the Kim & Jason comic strip and share the spirit of childhood. The two live in Madison, Wisconsin and enjoy long walks by the lake.

Jason grew up in Peru, Illinois, where he formulated an addiction to all things *Star Wars*. Some of his previous jobs include: keeping score for Little League games, washing cars for a GM dealership, assembling widgets at a nail factory, teaching college art history, and designing ad layouts for a small newspaper. He particularly enjoys superheroes, shrimp, Reese's peanut butter cups, Apple computers, ice cream cakes from Dairy Queen, listening to music, loitering at Barnes & Noble, visiting new places, and sugar-laden cereal.

As a professional speaker, Jason has the unique ability to connect with audiences of any age, and is just as comfortable with a classroom of kindergartners as he is in a meeting room with moms. By sharing personal experiences and lessons learned, Jason inspires audiences with his humorous anecdotes and unique childlike perspective. He is available for a limited number of seminars, conferences, annual meetings, keynotes, and workshops. Visit www.KimandJason.com for details.

If you liked this book, you'll **love** reading Jason's online blog, *Bird Droppings*. Check it out at **www.KimandJason.com/blog**

Kim & Jason ®

At its core, Kim & Jason *is all about helping grown-ups of all ages to Escape Adulthood, whether it's through a stress-reducing chuckle or a nostalgic reflection at a treasured childhood memory. But just as importantly, we are extremely passionate about making a difference in the lives of children as well.*

A good childhood is a precious thing, something every person deserves. Childhood is threatened every day by things like poverty, disease, and abuse. We're committed to doing what we can to help ensure that kids growing up today have wonderful childhoods to look back on tomorrow. That's why we pledge 3% of all merchandise sales to organizations that help meet the needs and improve the lives of children all over the world. Kim & Jason *readers have played a big role in helping to save childhood for kids everywhere.*

We hope that Kim & Jason *will help you rediscover that joyful, magical, and innocent childlike spirit and inspire you to slow down to appreciate the things in life that really matter. Because it's never too late to have a second childhood.*

--Kim and Jason Kotecki

www.KimandJason.com

The fun and colorful web site is jam packed with nostalgic pieces of childhood. A Kim & Jason *comic appears daily and the site has a number of other intriguing features:*

Get Kim & Jason *FREE by E-Mail!

• **Club K&J:** Sign up to receive *Kim & Jason* by e-mail. It's FREE and you'll get behind the scenes news, sneak previews, and special offers.

• **The Lemonade Stand:** Lots of cool products are available from the Kim & Jason Collection, including vibrant matted and framed artwork, books, greeting cards, candles, mugs, and various wearables like T-shirts and hats. With the growing popularity of the internationally-known strip, select retailers are now carrying merchandise from the Kim & Jason Collection. Check out KimandJason.com/lemonade_stand for a list of K&J retailers in your neck of the woods.

• **FUNdraising:** Sell *Kim & Jason* goodies to raise big bucks for your school or organization.

• **The Chalkboard:** Share your own childhood stories and read what others have written.

• **eCard Zone:** A vast collection of e-cards are available to send to friends and family, colleagues and clients.

• **Publish K&J:** Ask us how you can publish *Kim & Jason* in your newspaper, newsletter, or web site.

• **Guest Speaking:** Jason is available for a limited number of professional speaking presentations and seminars.

Give the gift of *Escape Adulthood* to your family, friends, and business associates. Check with your favorite bookstore or order here:

☐ YES, I want ____ copies of *Escape Adulthood* at $14.95 each, plus shipping. (*$2 for first book, $1 for each additional book. Please add 5.5% sales tax for books shipped to WI addresses.*)

☐ YES, I want to receive *Kim & Jason* comics FREE by e-mail. My e-mail address is listed below.

☐ YES, I am interested in having Jason Kotecki speak to my organization. Please contact me with details.

Please charge my:
☐ Visa   ☐ Mastercard   ☐ Check Enclosed

Credit Card # _____
Expiration date (month/year) _____/_____
Name _____
Organization _____
Address _____
City _____ State _____ ZIP _____
Phone _____ Fax _____
E-mail (please print clearly) _____
Signature X_____

Return to:
JBiRD iNK, Ltd.
535 Moorland Rd. Suite #203 Madison, WI 53713

Order online at: www.EscapeAdulthood.com